THE GLASTONBURY LEGENDS

A view of the ruins of the Abbey Church

THE GLASTONBURY
LEGENDS

*Joseph of Arimathea, The Holy Grail
and King Arthur*

*

R. F. TREHARNE

THE CRESSET PRESS

Printed in Great Britain by
Western Printing Services Ltd, Bristol

To my daughter Elizabeth

CONTENTS

ILLUSTRATIONS

PREFACE

THIS BOOK makes no pretence to being a work of
original or independent research: its debt to the much
earlier works of Professor W. W. Newell and the late
Dean Armitage Robinson will be immediately obvious to
any reader who knows them. I have drawn unhesitatingly
and copiously from these and from a few others of the works
listed in my bibliography, notably from Mr. Lewis Thorpe's
new translation of *Geoffrey of Monmouth's History of the Kings
of Britain*, Sir Thomas Kendrick's *British Antiquity*, Grahame
Clark's *Prehistoric England* and Professor H. E. Butler's
Autobiography of Gerald of Wales, and I acknowledge gratefully my debt to these several authors. In fact, this is a
work of synthesis and, to some extent, of re-interpretation,
intended not for the specialist in any aspect of this many-
sided subject, but for the general reader interested in the
Glastonbury Legends and their meaning. Professor Newell's
long article, written more than sixty years ago, is buried
in the files of the publications of an American learned
society, and there can be extremely few copies of it available even in academic libraries in this country. Dean
Armitage Robinson's delightful little book, published more
than thirty years ago, has long been out of print and there
is, I understand, no thought of re-printing it. Moreover,
in the intervening years a great deal has been published
which, although it does not alter any of the essential conclusions put forward in those two works, makes it possible
to carry the story somewhat further, to state both evidence
and findings more positively, and above all to provide a
much wider and fuller background to the story and so to

ix

help the reader to understand how these legends came into being and grew. The widespread and perennial interest in the Glastonbury Legends, together with the added information now available, is, I hope, a sufficient justification of this attempt to re-examine their historical validity, and to set them in this wider background. I can only ask forgiveness from the devout believers in the full legend of Joseph of Arimathea and King Arthur at Glastonbury, and express the hope that however destructive the iconoclastic hands of the historian may seem, they have not been either impious or irreverent.

My particular thanks are due to the Rev. Trevor Jalland, D.D., for his persistent urging that I should write up for publication the lecture which, at his suggestion, I was invited to give at the Glastonbury Pilgrimage in 1960, and to Mr. W. Synge for the invitation to turn the lecture into a book for The Cresset Press and for the immense trouble which he has personally taken to obtain the best possible photographs and blocks for the illustrations. I must also thank my College for the arrangements which allowed my departmental secretary, Mrs. C. O'Toole, to type the manuscript for me. To my wife the deepest thanks are due for her encouragement during a long spell of illness and convalescence, for her help and criticism with the final typescript and for the labour of compiling the index.

R. F. TREHARNE

University College of Wales,
Aberystwyth, December 1966.

I

IN AN ENGLAND which is ceasing to be, in any but a
nominal sense, a Christian country, the yearly Glastonbury Pilgrimage is an impressive and a significant
demonstration of the fact that to many thousands of Eng-
lishmen and Englishwomen the faith of their fathers is still
their way of life. Impressive and significant whether the
beholder shares or understands the faith of the pilgrims or
whether he does not—it is a specifically Anglican, and, on
the whole, a High Anglican demonstration—the onlooker,
whatever his own form of Christian attachment or even if
he has none at all, cannot watch unimpressed. It is not a
spontaneous demonstration, but an organized—indeed, a
very well organized—public witness of the faith of those
who make the pilgrimage and march in the great procession. But organized though it is, largely by the high dignitaries of the Church of England in the South-West, it
evokes every year such a massive and devoted response
from the laity to whom the organizers have appealed, that
the strength and depth of feeling which moves the pilgrims
to their march gives to the Pilgrimage all the sense of spon-
taneity which the organizers could wish to evoke. The Pilgrimage, year by year, is not just a matter of a single procession and a speedy return home: it is a sustained, long and
varied demonstration, even, for many who come, an act of
self-dedication. By rail, bus, coach and car, by bicycle and
even on foot, thousands of pilgrims pour into Glastonbury

on a Friday evening and a Saturday morning late in June, when summer is at its height. There are special services in the great, airy fifteenth-century parish church of St. John, and in the chapel of St. Mary in the ruined Abbey, including of course early morning communion in the lower storey of the Chapel, recently re-dedicated to St. Joseph. There is a fairly stiff full-length academic lecture delivered in St. John's church, to a packed audience of many hundreds, by a professional scholar who treats his chosen subject as he would a foundation lecture in the great hall of his own University. Most important of all is the great procession which winds its slow way from the Parish Church through the main streets of the little town to the Abbey grounds, to hear yet another service there, with an address by one of the bishops. While for most of the pilgrims it means one long day of travel, procession, services and return home, for hundreds it occupies the whole week-end. The atmosphere of the Pilgrimage is not that of the gala-day of festivities which we expect of a parish field-day, with its 'walking', its Sunday-school treat and its games: without any touch of sadness, self-mortification or mourning, it is a solemn and sober, disciplined witness of conviction and faith.

Nowhere is this better seen or felt than in the great procession, in which all the pilgrims march; all is discipline, order, decorum and self-restraint. Led by the prelates and the high dignitaries of the Church, diocese by diocese and parish by parish, in organized and solemn dignity the thousands of pilgrims from all over the South-West, from Cornwall to Hampshire, Wiltshire and Somerset, march slowly past. As they march they sing the great processional hymns of the Christian Church, kept in time and tune by scores of loud-speakers relaying the organ-music from the parish church. Hundreds of silken and embroidered banners, from

2

diocese, archdeaconry and parish in turn, proclaim the widespread response of the whole South-West to the Pilgrimage, and bear aloft a stream of rich colour. The copes and vestments of the clergy, splendid with gorgeous fabrics and embroidery, and the robes of the singing choirs give to the Pilgrimage a magnificence which is but rarely equalled by the often tawdry finery of similar processions on the Continent: this is splendour perfectly tended and magnificence well-groomed. Yet, even more than the superb display of the clergy with their somewhat too studied piety of demeanour, it is the marching laity who most impress. The clergy, after all, are professionals in their processions, and they enact their part as professionals should; but the laity are here as themselves, whether as individuals or as companies of parishioners, and they have neither professional training nor magnificence of vestments to sustain them in their demeanour. On they come, parish after parish, behind their parish banner, their priest and their choir. Some are obviously well-to-do, but most are humble folk, not rich in this world's goods, bearing witness to the faith that is in them. Many are obviously tired from long journeying: some have small children clinging to their hands, some even push baby-carriages bearing children too small to walk. At moments the sight has more than a touch of pathos: but it never loses its simple and impressive dignity, springing from the affirmation of faith which is the sole reason for their marching, singing presence. Only a cynic or an embittered foe of Christianity could watch unimpressed and unsympathetic.

That such an annual demonstration should be organized by the Anglican Church is not in itself startling or unexpected, though the extent of the region on which it draws and the size and quality of the response, year after year, are a significant matter of remark. But why has Glastonbury

3

been chosen as the scene for this great demonstration, and why is it Glastonbury every year? Glastonbury is not, and in historic time never has been, the seat of a bishopric. Nor, on the other hand, is the present-day Glastonbury Pilgrimage either a continuance or a revival of any similar gathering of religious witness in early or medieval times. It is a wholly modern and recent innovation, in that sense (but only in that sense) artificial, which has taken root and flourished mightily because it has appealed, not only to a deep and abiding general religious conviction, but because it taps a powerful spring of Christian tradition which makes Glastonbury unique in the Christian beliefs of thousands of people in the South-West, and which therefore makes Glastonbury the only possible site for such a religious demonstration as is this Pilgrimage.

It is nothing less than the widespread belief, by no means a monopoly of high Anglicans only, that it was to Glastonbury, first of all places in these islands of ours, that the Christian faith first came, and that Glastonbury is therefore the fountain and head-spring of Christianity in England, and indeed, in the whole of the British Isles. Those who hold to this tradition—and they are many thousands — believe devoutly that, some thirty years after the Crucifixion, St. Joseph of Arimathea and a band of missionary disciples came to Britain and chose Glastonbury to be the first abiding-place of Christianity in these islands, and that he erected here the first Christian church in Britain. There are even some who believe that it was Christ himself who, with his own hands, built this first of all Christian churches in Britain, and that St. Joseph, when he came, came to restore and perpetuate what Christ had begun. It is this belief that was the inspiration of William Blake's great Christian hymn, 'Jerusalem': the 'mountains green' on which 'those feet in ancient times' walked, were the hills

4

around Glastonbury, and 'England's pleasant pastures' on which 'the holy Lamb of God was seen' were the level meadows which now surround the little town, though in Christ's lifetime the local scene was utterly different. It is this tradition which makes Glastonbury the scene of the annual Pilgrimage of the South-West, and it is this belief, in one or the other of its variant forms, that explains the extraordinary appeal and response of the Pilgrimage in our own days.

The Glastonbury Legend asserts that the Christian faith was brought by St. Joseph of Arimathea in the year A.D. 63 (or even earlier, between A.D. 40 and 50, as one version claims). Joseph had been sent by his friend and leader, the Apostle Philip, who had just completed the conversion of Gaul, to carry the faith to the neighbouring Britons. Accompanied by a band of followers, he brought with him the Holy Grail, the sacred chalice of the Last Supper, which Pontius Pilate had given to him, and in which, at the Crucifixion, he had collected Christ's blood, which had remained miraculously uncorrupted throughout his long journeyings. After many perils and adventures, Joseph and his companions landed somewhere in South-Western Britain, possibly on the Somerset coast, and made their way eastwards towards Glastonbury Tor, without attempting to find any earlier abiding-place. At length, approaching the Tor across the marsh, all weary with their long journeying, they rested on the rise about a mile to the south-west of Glastonbury, and ever since their halting-place has been called 'Wearyall Hill'. At the foot of the Tor, St. Joseph stopped to pray: before he knelt, he thrust his staff into the ground, and lo!, a miracle! The staff immediately took root and budded; it was a sign from heaven that he had reached Journey's End.

And so, in honour and imitation of Christ's twelve

disciples, St. Joseph decreed that the place where he had knelt should be for ever dedicated to the worship of Christ, and that twelve of his companions should live together there, below the Tor, as a community of hermits to ensure the perpetuation of worship on this holy spot. At the bidding and under the guidance of St. Gabriel, the disciples built there the '*Vetusta Ecclesia*', the 'Ancient Church', the first Christian church to be built in Britain, and so, the fountain-head of our faith. For this reason, and to mark its eternal primacy, Christ himself came and dedicated the church to his Holy Mother: indeed, one version of the story is that the disciples found the church already built for them on the spot, 'erected by no human hands', but made by Christ himself, the carpenter's son. It was a primitive little 'church of boughs', of wattle and daub on a timber frame, poor and humble as was fitting for the church of God who was born man in a manger and who spent his life in humility among the poor: but it was to become the holy of holies of Glastonbury, the most sacred shrine in Britain, renovated and devotedly preserved by the monks of Glastonbury until, alas, fire destroyed it in 1184. St. Joseph's rooted staff became the famous Glastonbury Thorn, flowering every year at Christmas in honour of Christ's birth, until it was cut down and burnt by a Puritan fanatic in the seventeenth century, and even now succeeded by a slip of its own stock, which defies unbelief by continuing to flower unseasonably, as the parent tree had flowered before it. Near the foot of the Tor St. Joseph eventually buried the Holy Grail lest rude hands should profane it; in modern times 'Chalice Well' has been pointed out as the place of its burial, though the Grail has never been found.

Yet the Grail has not lacked seekers. Why else is it that, according to the other branch of the Glastonbury legend,

King Arthur and his knights, devoted to the endless search for the Holy Grail, are especially located here in Glastonbury and its neighbourhood? For Glastonbury is the Isle of Avalon, to which, after his last fatal battle on the River Camlan, King Arthur was by magic 'borne away for the healing of his wounds'. Pomparlès, the 'Bridge Perilous', where Arthur threw his mighty sword Excalibur into the water, and the mysterious arm rose up to grasp it and to draw it down out of sight, is the bridge over the little River Brue, where the road from Glastonbury to the west, through Street, leaves the town and crosses the stream. And Camelot, Arthur's city and stronghold, is Cadbury Castle, lying some twelve miles away to the south-east—an Iron Age B contour hill fort, to give it a technical archaeological description, lying near the long prehistoric trackway which, beginning near Ilchester, crosses Southern England by way of Salisbury Plain and the chalk scarp of the North Downs, to reach the coast near Dover. This three-sided fortress, guarded by four huge banks and deep ditches, is the most tremendous prehistoric camp in Somerset, and one of the mightiest in all Britain; it is typical of the new style of fortification, by which defence in depth was secured by the multiplication of banks and ditches, whereby, near the end of the Iron Age, the inhabitants of south-western Britain tried to defend themselves from a new menacing invasion from the Continent. Mrs. Jacquetta Hawkes has described it as 'one of the most magnificent hill forts in the West Country . . . whose four lines of powerful ramparts . . . are cut from the rock and in places have dry-stone masonry still intact on their inner face: sometimes the crest of a wall, even in its present tumbled state, stands more than forty feet above the bottom of its ditch'.* The

* Jacquetta Hawkes, *A Guide to the Prehistoric and Roman Monuments in England and Wales*, p. 145.

scene, according to legend, of one of the greatest of Arthur's victories over the encroaching Saxons, it is a worthy site, even though a prehistoric camp resembles not at all a fortress-city in a medieval romance, to serve as the location of Tennyson's 'many-towered Camelot', and the identification is supported by the presence of 'Arthur's Well' and 'Arthur's Causeway' near-by.

And should any lingering doubt still vex us, was it not, about 1191, as a result of an ancient Welsh bard's prophecy, and later of a vision vouchsafed to one of the Glastonbury monks, in the consecrated burial-ground of the Abbey that the bodies of King Arthur and Queen Guinevere were discovered, buried deep in the sacred earth between two mysterious ancient pyramids, and identified by a leaden cross bearing, in Latin, the inscription 'Here lies buried the renowned King Arthur, with Guinevere his second wife, in the Isle of Avalon'—an inscription not only identifying the remains of the King, but also revealing that Avalon and Glastonbury are one and the same? And so, by the last stage in the linking of the two Glastonbury legends, the Holy Grail, hidden by St. Joseph, becomes the mystic object of the quest of King Arthur's Knights of the Round Table, so that saint and kingly hero are made the joint supporters of the glory of Glastonbury's ancient shrine.

Of course, the identification of Arthur's 'Camelot' with Cadbury Castle, and the locating of his tragic last battle near Glastonbury, on the utterly insignificant little river Brue, are powerfully challenged by other and stronger claims—if indeed we are, for a moment, to take seriously the age-long attempts of men to find real sites for these imaginary places from a faery world of myth and legend. Cadbury Castle was constructed long before the Romans conquered Britain, and many centuries before the time of the historic

8

Arthur, if such a leader there ever was in history. Excavations conducted in the summer of 1966 by Mr. Leslie Alcock have abundantly confirmed earlier indications that the fortress was reoccupied in the turbulent centuries following the collapse of Roman rule in Britain, and have greatly strengthened, without definitively proving, the local tradition that Cadbury Castle was at least one of Arthur's strongholds, if not his headquarters. It should, however, be remembered that the Saxons did not penetrate into this part of Somerset until more than a century after Arthur's time, and that it is highly unlikely that Arthur fought any of his battles with the Saxons in or near this great fortress. This matter will be discussed more fully at the appropriate place in our argument. Geoffrey of Monmouth, the first narrator of Arthur's legendary reign and exploits, would afford a very strong case for locating 'Camelot' at the great legionary Roman fortress of Caerleon on Usk, where Arthur, he says, held his majestic court. Alternatively Geoffrey could be used to make almost as strong a case for placing 'Camelot' at Tintagel, towering high on its superb cliff above the restless Atlantic, and not very far from the river Camel where Geoffrey himself locates Arthur's last battle, in a local topography which accords, far better than anything which Glastonbury can offer, with Geoffrey's description of the scene.

Even so, no other place in all Britain but Glastonbury has ever claimed to be the 'Isle of Avalon', and even more surely no other spot claims to be the first abiding-place in Britain of St. Joseph of Arimathea, or the site of the first Christian church in Britain, and the starting-point of the Christian faith in our land. In these two respects the Glastonbury legends have no contenders against their claims. These, then, are the Glastonbury legends, which we propose to investigate. It is a delicate task, for we are

9

dealing with the cherished beliefs of very many devout Christians, and while of course this particular tradition is no essential part of the Christian faith, to those who believe it to be true, it has been and still is a powerful inspiration and comfort. Beliefs such as this cannot be treated lightly; yet the historian has his duty, which is to discover and to reveal the truth, if his historical science and technique enable him to do so, to the best of his ability, even if this may mean laying what may seem to be sacrilegious hands on devoutly held beliefs. It is exactly this task that we have set ourselves.

II

Bᴇғᴏʀᴇ ᴡᴇ ᴄᴀɴ examine the Glastonbury Legends, we must first glance at the topography of Glastonbury itself and of the land around it, and we must also look at the early history of the district, from late prehistoric times down to the English conquest and settlement of Somerset, and at the subsequent destiny of Glastonbury under Saxon rule. This is necessary, not merely as a helpful setting and background for a study of the Legends, but because all of these things, local topography, prehistory, and the development of Glastonbury in late Celtic and in Saxon times, enter into the very essence of the Glastonbury Legends, making their birth possible and shaping their astonishing growth. And since Glastonbury Tor is at the very heart of the Legends, with the Tor we will begin.

Glastonbury Tor might have been designed by nature for the site of an ancient, holy legend touching the very heart of the mysteries of religion and faith. The Tor is the scarped end of a low ridge running almost east and west from the southern end of the Mendips, not completely continuous throughout its length, but rising at its westernmost tip to over 400 feet, where it ends abruptly with a steep western face plunging down into the Marsh at its foot. Not only this western end, but the northern and southern faces too are steep, and the ridge everywhere narrow. Level, even fields and osier-beds, low-lying, and lush through modern drainage, surround the Tor on all sides, so that even to-day, topographically speaking, it has an air of isolated singularity. In primitive times, before the Marsh was drained, it was a real island in 'a fresh-water marsh with a thick growth of willow, alder and hazel, among which, in the pools, grew the bog-bean, water-lilies, spearwort and pond-weed'.* The Bristol Channel then reached deep into the heart of Somerset, flooding all the lowlands between the Mendips and the Quantock Hills with shallow tidal waters or with thick, almost impenetrable swamp, as far as the present sites of Ilchester and Crewkerne: from out of this primitive jungle the ridges of the Polden Hills and of Glastonbury Tor stood up like island reefs above the swamps. To-day, admittedly, the tower of the ruined thirteenth-century Chapel of St. Michael, built on the very summit of the Tor, helps greatly to single out for the roving eye this particular eminence from the other hills and ridges of this part of Somerset. Erect like a great monument or landmark on the apex of the ridge, the tower now emphasizes the character of the Tor as a dramatic natural feature, drawing one's gaze almost everywhere in the surrounding countryside, high or low, wherever an open view can be found. But even before the tower was built, the Tor itself, in its natural state, must always have been the eye-compelling feature of this countryside of strangely contrasted hills and swampy levels.

The first known prehistoric remains in the land immediately around the Tor may go back beyond 400 B.C., but the famous 'lake villages' of the Dobunni at Glastonbury and Meare, 'permanent settlements in a region half-swamp, half actual lake . . . [amid] dreary marshes, the haunt of pelican and cormorant, heron, bittern, wild duck, swan and crane',† were probably built about 50 B.C., perhaps by Armorican refugees fleeing from Caesar's ruthless

* Stuart Piggott, *British Prehistory*, p. 173.   † *Ibid.*

conquest of Armorica (Brittany) in 56 B.C., though one authority at least attributes their foundation to Dumnonian colonists coming from Cornwall or Devon along the Bristol Channel, and finding their way inland along the river Brue about 150 B.C.

The later Iron Age, and especially the two centuries before the Roman conquest, was a time of strife and danger, when the stronger tribes raided, plundered and slaughtered their neighbours with ever-increasing savagery, and the powerful, well-equipped and aggressive Belgae crossed from north-eastern Gaul and slowly mastered the whole of south-eastern Britain with a ruthless militarism appropriate to a race of mixed Germanic and Celtic stock, as Caesar described them. Many of the native Britons reoccupied the old Bronze Age hill-forts of the south-west, powerfully strengthening their earlier defences by adding two or even three lines of walls and ditches, and planning complex and cunningly defended entrances, as at Cadbury Castle and Maiden Hill. But the communities which established themselves near Glastonbury found a different, and perhaps a better way of self-defence: they took refuge in the swamps, using water and marsh instead of hill-top forts, for protection. A mile north of Glastonbury, and two miles farther on to the north-west at Meare, the British peoples of this district, whether with or without the leadership of refugees from Armorica, grouped themselves into two communities and built themselves villages in the shallow waters near the edge of a large freshwater lake, not far from the higher ground on which they tilled their fields and grazed their herds and flocks, but so sited that the lake and the marshes afforded them broad and effective natural moats. At both places the villages were built on an artificial island (*crannog* or *terpen*). At Glastonbury this was an elaborately-constructed and well-made triangular platform resting on

13

a firm foundation of stones, faggots, brushwood, rushes and peat laid on the bed of the mere: it was nearly four acres in area, and its outer edges were bound by a strong casing of great logs laid horizontally and mortised into strong piles driven into the bed of the mere, with frequent offsets laid at right angles to resist the outward lateral pressure of the platform, while the vertical piles were frequently renewed as the weight of the whole structure showed signs of producing too much outward spread. The outer edge of the 'island' was defended by a strong palisade of tough wicker-work hurdles of timber and brushwood linking together a close-set line of vertical poles varying from five to fourteen feet in height above the platform, according to the degree of protection thought necessary for each section of the defence. Outside the palisade, on the north-east side, a forty-yard stone and clay causeway, kept in position by horizontal timber planks and hurdles fixed to vertical piles, and protected by a parallel breakwater of large stones, led to a wooden landing-stage which projected into deeper, open water, thus providing moorings for the heavy twenty-foot dug-out canoes (one of which was found in place by modern excavators), in which these amphibious villagers ventured cautiously on their coastal journeys along the shores of the Bristol Channel, and even, in favourable weather, crossed the dangerous open waters to the South Wales coast.

On the Glastonbury 'island' were built eighty-nine circular huts, varying from eighteen to twenty-eight feet in diameter, with small projecting vestibules closed by strong double swing-doors made of oak. Each hut was built on a heavy timber foundation of parallel logs held together by frequently renewed concentric rings of piles driven into the bed of the mere around the edge of the foundation. A layer of clay, placed on the timber foundation and paved with split wooden floor-boards, formed the floor of the hut:

14

The prehistoric lake village—Glastonbury

(Somerset County Museum, Taunton)

An aerial view of Cadbury Castle

(Dr. J. K. St. Joseph)

fresh layers of clay and new floor-boards were put down on top of the old as the weight of the hut caused the underlying peat bed of the mere to sink, and as many as ten successive floors might accumulate on top of one another in a single hut. A hearth of baked clay or of lias slabs lay near the centre of the hut, and was renewed every time a new floor was laid, or even more frequently, since it was the point which, in the whole floor, weighed most heavily upon the foundation: thirteen hearths were found one above the other in a single hut. Dome-shaped clay ovens have been found inside the huts. The huts themselves seem to have been lightly constructed above the floor-level, partly to avoid additional weight on the foundation, and partly to allow easy dismantling and re-erection whenever a new floor had to be laid: the roof was probably a conical reed thatch supported by the outer wall and a centre pole. Assuming that all the huts at Glastonbury were occupied simultaneously, this could easily allow for a population of 500: at Meare, which was probably constructed earlier than the Glastonbury lake village, there were two crannogs each carrying about sixty huts, which would mean a population of 600 or more. It will readily be seen that, for their age and sites, these were two large communities, even though now little remains to show how busy they were, save for a few low and irregularly shaped mounds and banks in the uneven fields of a marshy hollow; the prehistoric mere itself has shrunk, thanks to modern drainage, to a narrow ditch called the 'Old Rhyne'.

Yet here, in their days of prosperity, lived two flourishing communities engaged in agriculture, industry, and long-distance trade. The extent and the detail of our knowledge of them we owe to the fortunate circumstance that they were founded on peat which eventually engulfed and covered them, for the peat has preserved foodstuffs, implements, pottery, carpentry, basketwork and metalwork with little serious damage to the appearance, colour and construction of the material, whereas the soils which cover most prehistoric sites have often reduced the original object to something which in texture, shape and colour is unrecognizable save to a trained archaeologist. Here then, thanks to this local circumstance and to the long and skilful excavations of Dr. A. H. Bulleid and Mr. H. St. George Gray, we can reconstruct in exceptional detail the life and work of these highly capable and artistic people who lived near Glastonbury two thousand years ago. For basic subsistence they relied on a systematic and well-developed husbandry, growing barley, wheat, peas and beans, collecting blackberries, sloes and haws in season to supplement their diet, and even using carraway and poppy seeds to flavour their somewhat dull cereal foods. They stored their grain in circular pits eight or nine feet deep and from three to five feet across, lined with plaited straw or reeds, and entered by runged wooden ladders: every five years or so they had to dig new silos because the old pits had become foul and stale. They had herds of short-horned cattle, which they knew how to poll, and large flocks of slender, large-horned sheep: they also kept pigs, goats, dogs and horses. They gathered the honey of wild bees, and used slings to kill the abundant water-fowl of the swamps—pelicans, cranes, swans and ducks. They fished with weighted nets for roach, perch, shad and trout, and they sometimes speared pike and salmon, perhaps at night with the aid of torches or flares. They used both spear and sling—rarely arrows—for hunting the deer, the fox, the otter, the beaver and the wild cat, whether for food or fur. Their iron tools, complete with gracefully shaped yet highly efficient wooden handles, have been recovered intact. To transport their crops and other loads by land, they used carts drawn on wheels nearly three feet across, with twelve spokes skil-fully fitted into a strong wooden axle-box; wooden sledges were also used on waterlogged ground where a wheeled cart might easily get foundered.

The men of Glastonbury and Meare were obviously ex-pert carpenters—their handling of timber in constructing their artificial 'islands', with their causeways and landing-stages, and in flooring their huts would prove this, even without the much more precise carpentry required for their well-built carts, wheels, loom-frames and other heavy woodwork. But their light woodwork is even more impres-sive in its style and natural grace, combined with admir-able functional efficiency—the well-balanced and shapely wooden handles for their iron tools, and still more their perfectly turned wooden bowls, tubs and spoons, the earli-est lathe-turned utensils so far found in Britain, made with a technique which survives unchanged in Wales to-day. These lighter articles are beautifully decorated with elegant flowing incised patterns, abstract in character and owing nothing to Roman or Greek naturalism, which were adap-ted from the Continental La Tène style via Brittany, and developed here in south-western Britain into the Late Celtic curvilinear style which is their special contribution to Celtic art. These men were craftsmen and artists at once, and their work is still a joy to see. In making hurdles, wicker-work and baskets, usually from osiers, their skill was such that much of what the modern excavators have found is, when cleaned, indistinguishable in technique, pattern and quality from the best basket and wicker-work done by their successors in the same place to-day. They spun and wove their own wool, as leaden spindle-whorls and loom-weights, bone combs, and portions of loom-frames plainly show, though none of their fabrics have so far been discovered.

17

But it was in metal-work and in pottery that their blending of technical skill and artistic sensibility reached its highest and most mature development. They used a great range of metals, as their surviving forges, furnaces and crucibles show. They imported ingots of wrought iron from the Forest of Dean, partly in the form of the clumsy 'currency bars' used until the British kingdoms began to make coins on Roman and Greek models, but mainly for fashioning into a wide variety of implements, tools and weapons of the most advanced design—knives, bill-hooks, chisels, gouges and even saws; adzes, axe-heads and swords, the last sometimes beautifully decorated on the hilts and scabbards. It has been remarked that some of this iron-work differs only slightly from the hand-made wrought iron implements that were made at country smithies in the last century, before mass-production wiped out the individual blacksmith. They worked lead, from the near-by Mendips, into a great variety of utensils, though they do not seem to have learnt the art of extracting silver from lead. Tin was brought from Cornwall, and copper from still further afield, and they worked both metals into small ornaments, but of course their main use for them was to manufacture bronze, the medium where their artistry appears at its best in finely shaped and exquisitely decorated bowls, mirrors, brooches and bracelets, harness and many other things. In this medium again the graceful abstract curves and patterns of Late Celtic art show to the fullest advantage, and it seems certain that the use of these designs in both woodwork and pottery was originally an imitation of their metalwork. They had even mastered the difficult art of enamelling, and had learnt how to apply the enamel in fused state to exactly those portions of the bronze surface which the design required. As potters they showed remarkable powers of rapid development in both technique and taste in the short period for which they inhabited their lake-villages. Their earliest pottery was hand-made, and decorated with the geometrical patterns inherited from the Bronze Age: but long before the end they were producing wheel-made pottery, decorated in the characteristic flowing style of Late Celtic abstract art, the finest and best pre-Roman pottery in Britain. They were skilled glass-workers too, as is proved by their clear glass beads decorated with delightful inlaid patterns of chrome yellow threads: amber beads and personal ornaments of Kimmeridge shale, imported from Dorsetshire, together with small ornaments made of polished bone, further testify to the range of their skill and artistry.

The two lake villages were also a centre of long-distance trade, possibly the most important in Britain at this time. We have seen that the villagers imported tin from Cornwall, iron from the Forest of Dean, copper almost certainly from far overseas, and Kimmeridge shale from the Dorset coast, as well as amber from remote sources, perhaps as far away as the Baltic shores. They worked up this material into the implements, utensils and ornaments described above, and while much of this manufacture was put to local use, a large surplus was exported over the whole of the wide area from which the imports were drawn, and to places yet still farther away. Archaeological finds of bronze bowls and mirrors, glass beads, and even of pottery made at Glastonbury— and this at a time when pottery was very rarely carried far afield by prehistoric traders—show the extent of this export trade, some of which reached Armorica, the shores of Cardigan Bay, and even northern Ireland. We should not assume that the lake-villagers themselves carried their trade-goods to all of these places, for in prehistoric times much trade necessarily depended on intermediate tribes and communities who bought goods to sell them again another stage farther on. But the big dug-out canoes, twenty feet long and skilfully make with all the carpentering techniques which the Glastonbury men had developed, were capable of long coastal voyages up and down the shores of the Bristol Channel, and even across that tricky stretch of water to the South Wales coast, and we need not doubt that they made such trading voyages as often as the weather and the seasons would permit, rather than share the profits of their trade with intermediate tribes and communities. Not unfairly, therefore, have these two villages been described as 'a great Celtic emporium'.

Altogether, this astonishing mass of detailed information which modern archaeologists have been able to recover to show us how the Glastonbury-Meare communities lived, indicates plainly that in an age of ever-growing violence and strife they were able to exist for at least a century as a prosperous agricultural and industrial community, peaceful and unaggressive by habit and interest, able to develop their material civilization to a height which made them the leading cultural influence in south-western Britain. Several scholars have described them, therefore, as possessing 'by far the most advanced civilization by that time in this country'. But we must remember that the peculiar physical and chemical conditions which have preserved the Glastonbury 'finds' in such unusually good condition and complete state may easily give us a false impression of the uniqueness of the material culture of these two communities, and Mrs. Jacquetta Hawkes has rightly cautioned us that the special culture which they represent, though unquestionably unique in Britain at that time, may in fact have been spread over a considerably wider area, as the common possession of the whole kingdom of the Dobunni (centred on the later cantonal capital of Cirencester), to which, politically, Glastonbury and Meare had become attached, and possibly even to their southern neighbours, the Durotriges of South Somerset and Dorset. Even so, Glastonbury and Meare must have been the chief economic and trading focus of this flourishing south-western civilization.

But they enjoyed their peace and prosperity under constant and ever-growing menace: not for nothing had they built their laboriously constructed islands and sought safety in cramped, unhealthy and uncomfortable quarters which required constant renovation and repair to keep them from sinking into the swamps—a kind of British Venice in origin, and in way of life, though fated not to enjoy Venice's long history of success. Although the Dobunni were by no means completely defenceless before their less civilized and highly dangerous neighbours, the Silures of south-east Wales and the savage Belgae who conquered the whole of south-east England, the Dobunni suffered much from these powerful warrior tribes. While the Silures were satisfied to raid and plunder their richer neighbours, the Belgae sought nothing less than complete conquest, with extermination or utter subjection of their victims: they were the Prussians of their time. For Glastonbury and Meare the end came suddenly, shortly before the middle of the first century A.D., and probably on the very eve of the Roman invasion. The Belgae raided the two villages in force and utterly destroyed Glastonbury, massacring most of its inhabitants, and though Meare still survived, it lived on only as a crippled, ruined community. The glory had departed, and the brilliant flowering of Late Celtic culture in the Glastonbury marshes came thus to its tragic end.

Within a very few years, however, an army of new and utterly different conquerors had overrun this region, for by A.D. 47 the Roman Conquest of Britain, launched four years earlier by the Emperor Claudius, had reached the line of the Fosse-way and had made it, for the time being, the temporary frontier of the new Roman province of Britannia, imposing the firm *pax Romana* on the crushed Belgae and their former victims alike. Not surprisingly, the Dobunni welcomed this new conquest and were given, for a while, the status of subject-allies of Rome, and soon afterwards the lake-villages of Glastonbury and Meare were abandoned by the remaining survivors for ever. Where they went we do not know, nor do we know anything of their subsequent history. There is nothing at all to prove that they moved only to less cramped, unhealthy, and difficult sites on the adjacent higher and drier grounds where their fields had lain, and for all that the archaeologist can tell us, the district around Glastonbury may have been altogether deserted and have become a primitive wilderness once more. A few miscellaneous Roman finds, of inconclusive significance, have been unearthed around Glastonbury, and three miles away, near Street, a small Roman villa has been discovered, another of the prosperous little group of Roman villas established in south Somerset around Ilchester, Somerton, and Ham. The name of Street itself recalls the existence of a Roman road which ran NNW from Ilchester by way of Somerton to Street, whence one fork went on north-west along the low, narrow ridge of the Polden Hills, while the other (conjectural only), may have crossed the Marsh by a now-vanished causeway running north to the important Mendip lead-mines at Charterhouse. But no Roman villa or permanent settlement of any kind has yet been unearthed at the foot of Glastonbury Tor, and the immediate vicinity may well have become utterly deserted, save for wandering hunters and fishermen, as being altogether too unattractive and inaccessible for the newly-Romanized Dobunni, who were quickly learning,

22

under the *pax Romana*, the delights of soft and civilized living. For the next six hundred years after the coming of the Romans, we know nothing whatsoever of the history of Glastonbury, by way of firm historical fact, except what we can gather from the traditions of Glastonbury Abbey itself. The Roman era and the sub-Roman period of the last revival of Celtic independence are alike blank so far as Glastonbury is concerned, except for the history of the Abbey itself. It is regarded by historians as reasonably certain that a Celtic monastery was established at Glastonbury, probably by wandering Irish missionaries in the sixth century, and there may well have been some sort of a primitive Christian shrine already on the spot long before the monastery was established, in fact, explaining why the monastery was established there: but this is only inference from the much later traditions which were firmly believed in the Abbey centuries afterwards. Until the whole of western Somerset passed into West Saxon hands after their victories at Bradford-on-Avon in 652 and at Penselwood in 658, inference and conjecture alone can furnish whatever history of Glastonbury we can discern, and the basis of our knowledge is entirely the tradition of Glastonbury Abbey.

From the English conquest and settlement of the district onwards, the history of Glastonbury, though at first a very slender thread, is continuous and unbroken, being the history of the Abbey down to its dissolution in 1539. King Ine of Wessex (A.D. 688–726) is often described as the founder of Glastonbury Abbey, but this is to ignore its earlier existence as a Celtic monastery long before Ine's time. We shall see that there can be no doubt whatsoever that when the West Saxons occupied the district soon after A.D. 568 they found an old and famous Celtic monastery already established and flourishing there, a shrine already

23

venerated by all the Christian British peoples as a place of awesome and holy antiquity. The West Saxons, themselves new converts to Christianity, willingly assumed the patronage and protection of so holy a place, and sought to turn its glory to their own fame. Ine indeed granted it such extensive possessions and privileges that he may fairly be said to have re-founded the Abbey by putting it on to a new and far more secure footing. Nevertheless, apart from lavish endowments, which cannot all be taken as genuine, and the names of the successive abbots (again not always reliable) we know remarkably little firm fact about the history of Glastonbury Abbey until in 940 the great Dunstan was made Abbot of Glastonbury by King Edmund. Under Dunstan Glastonbury became the power-house of the surging monastic revival in England in the middle and later years of the tenth century, the centre from which sprang the impetus which restored the late Anglo-Saxon church to its earlier glory, and ensured that the Benedictine rule of monasticism, with all that it stood for in the way of religious devotion, learning, order and sanity, would henceforth be the guiding light of all English monasticism.

And so, in English hands, Glastonbury became one of the very largest and wealthiest monastic houses in England, claiming in fact to be the premier monastery in the land. From its final completion early in the sixteenth century, Glastonbury certainly had the largest church in England, one of the largest in Europe, even. In the later middle ages the West Country folk had a slightly scandalous saying, that if the Abbot of Glastonbury were to marry to Abbess of Shaftesbury, they would be the richest pair in the kingdom. But Glastonbury's claim to be the premier English monastery rested neither on its size nor on its wealth: it sprang from Glastonbury's venerable tradition of supreme antiquity, an antiquity so great that its origins

24

really are lost in the mist of early time. Even that most strict and scrupulous of monastic historians, Professor David Knowles, allows that 'the original monastic foundation appears to date from the first half of the sixth century', an earlier origin than that which he accepts for any other English monastery; and he adds that 'some authorities claim that it was even earlier'.* If we understand the term 'monastic foundation' in its proper sense, an early sixth-century foundation is indeed much the most probable: but the tradition of the house traces its origin much farther back, claiming that Glastonbury is the oldest ecclesiastical site in England, possessing a continuous Christian tradition stretching unbroken from the Dissolution in 1539 back to the very beginning of Christianity in this land.

* David Knowles and R. Neville Hadcock, *Medieval Religious Houses; England and Wales*, p. 55, note.

III

WE HAVE NOW seen what are the legends which we seek to examine, and we have glanced briefly at the topographical setting and the early history of Glastonbury, before the time when the first attempt was made to set down the traditions in orderly form, and to attempt some examination of their credibility. How far back can we trace these legends? The earlier the origin of a legend, the greater the probability that it contains, concealed in its fantasy, at least some measure of truth. While great antiquity will not alone warrant the truth of a legend otherwise unsupported, a relatively late origin for a legend will at once arouse suspicion, especially if it can be shown that, at the earliest date to which it can be traced back, it was to the advantage of some person or of some organization that the legend should have been invented at that particular time in the particular circumstances then existing. Fortunately, we have an unusually good opportunity, not only of dating approximately the beginning of the Glastonbury legend, but also of reconstructing the particular contemporary circumstances of its birth. The opportunity is provided by two twelfth-century writers; William of Malmesbury, probably the greatest of all English historians writing in that century, in two works written during the later years of King Henry I, and Gerald of Wales, one of the most brilliant literary figures of the time of King Richard and King John.

William of Malmesbury had written a large-scale history of England, his great *De Gestis Regum Anglorum*, which he had finished in 1125; in the course of this book he had said that Glastonbury Abbey had been founded, on the advice of St. Aldhelm, by Ine, King of Wessex (688–726), a statement which he had repeated in his *De Gestis Pontificum Anglorum*, also finished in 1125. Critics evidently informed him that this, and other statements which he had made on the early history of Wessex, were mistaken and incomplete, and that he could rectify these errors by further research in the magnificent library and archives of Glastonbury, which contained very ancient documents unknown to William while he was preparing his *De Gestis Regum*. William, like the good historian he was, therefore visited Glastonbury to prepare a revised edition of the earlier portions of his great work, and he evidently found so much as to necessitate rewriting completely these earlier sections. In the course of another book, a *Life of St. Dunstan*, of uncertain date, it appears that at Glastonbury he has discovered new material which has convinced him of his error, in the first edition of the *De Gestis Regum*, in making Ine the founder of Glastonbury, and that he now realizes that Glastonbury was in fact very much older. Correcting the erroneous statement of Osbern, an earlier biographer of Dunstan, that Dunstan was the first Abbot of Glastonbury, he now says that 'Glastonbury had already passed under ecclesiastical authority long before the time of St. Patrick, who had died in A.D. 472'. In fact, he had been so impressed by what he had seen and heard at Glastonbury that he had decided to write a separate monograph on the antiquity of that great abbey, and in Book I of the *Life of Dunstan* he tells us that he has started writing this separate study, while in Book II he is able to say that he has now completed it, and he refers his readers to it for a fuller treatment of the

27

subject. As it can be shown that he was writing Book II of his *Life of Dunstan* not later than 1135, we can conclude that his visit to Glastonbury fell within the ten years, 1125–1135, and that his monograph on Glastonbury's history was written during that period, possibly before he had left Glastonbury to return to Malmesbury.

This monograph, the *De Antiquitate Glastoniensis Ecclesiae*, was both a courteous return to William's Glastonbury hosts for their hospitality and help, and also an expression of the tremendous impact which Glastonbury's documents, traditions and ancient remains had made on William's mind. What he had seen, read and heard at Glastonbury had convinced him, to use the words which he quoted from an alleged charter of re-foundation granted by King Ine, that Glastonbury 'was the first church in the Kingdom of Britain, and the source and fountain of all religion' in our land. He resolved to write a treatise which would take the origins of Glastonbury back to the very beginnings of Christianity in Britain, and recount the history of the venerable monastery from those origins down to his own day. It proved to be a noble *apologia* for Glastonbury and a handsome return for the kindness which the community had shown to him, both materially and by putting the resources of its library so fully at his disposal, and filling with oral tradition the gaps left by the Abbey's documents. What better return could the greatest English historian of his day have made?

William's monograph proved immensely gratifying to the pride of the Glastonbury monks, and they made full use of it. Many copies were made and put into circulation, and new editions were produced as needed in the succeeding decades. But gradually William's original treatise ceased to content the monks of Glastonbury, and although they would not forego the prestige of William's name on the title-page of their 'official' history, they began to alter his text. The alterations became more drastic as the later editions amplified William's story to support their growing pretensions, until the final version of the story, as we now possess it, became very different indeed from the much more cautious history which William had written.

The only manuscripts now surviving of the *De Antiquitate* are copies of the much-altered version as it stood about 1240/50, over a century after William's original, and they show what the Glastonbury community then believed—or, rather, what they wished others to believe—about the early history of Glastonbury Abbey. It is a very different and much more fabulous story than William's careful original had been. How, it may be asked, can we know this if the only surviving texts of the treatise are of the revised version of 1240/50? Fortunately, although no text of William's original monograph survives, we have a very full extract from it, made by William himself, containing all of the essential portions of what he had written on the origins and early history of Glastonbury. He wrote the monograph shortly before he rewrote the earlier sections of his *De Gestis Regum*, and he found that most of what he now wanted to say about the earlier history of Britain was derived from the documents which he had seen and the stories he had been told at Glastonbury. In fact, much of his revised version of the *De Gestis Regum* had to be written around the story of Glastonbury, and he saw no point in composing two differently-worded accounts of the same story based on the same source-materials. He therefore copied the whole of the relevant portions of the *De Antiquitate* into that part of the revised edition of the *De Gestis Regum Anglorum* which dealt with the history of Britain before the coming of the English, and with the early history of the Kingdom of Wessex. Thus, by comparing the relevant passages of William's revised *De Gestis Regum Anglorum* with the surviving texts of the much-altered *De Antiquitate Glastoniensis Ecclesiae*, we can see what William himself had written *c.* 1130 and what the Glastonbury monks were saying just over 100 years later. The comparison is very revealing.

Finally, Gerald of Wales, writing near the end of the century, provides an invaluable account of certain sensational happenings at Glastonbury, of which he was almost an eyewitness, which afford the clue for understanding how and why William's original story had been so drastically altered in the space of just over 100 years.

First let us summarize what is told in the final, much-altered version of the *De Antiquitate* current *c.* 1240. It tells that the Apostle Philip, having converted Gaul to Christianity, decided to send a mission over to Britain, so he ordained twelve of his disciples for this purpose and put them under the charge of St. Joseph of Arimathea. In the fifteenth year of the Assumption of the Blessed Virgin Mary (i.e. in A.D. 63) the disciples reached Britain and began their preaching. Arviragus, the heathen king of the Britons, though rejecting their gospel, was so impressed by their bearing and way of life that he gave them as their dwelling-place the district called by the British Ynys Witrin, the firm land around the foot of Glastonbury Tor, a desert place surrounded by swamp and forest, on which, much later, Glastonbury was to stand. Two subsequent pagan kings confirmed Arviragus' grant, adding further gifts so that in all there was one hide for each disciple—the 'Twelve Hides of Glastonbury' of medieval times. Presently St. Gabriel visited the brethren, and instructed them to erect, on a spot which he indicated, a 'church of boughs'; and since this was the first Christian church ever erected in the land, Christ himself honoured it by dedicating it to his

Mother. In this holy place, devoting themselves to fasting, watches and prayer, the twelve disciples lived as hermits in the wilderness; the Blessed Virgin often appeared to them, exhorting them, comforting them and supplying their material needs so long as they lived. But after the last of them had died, the site became deserted, a refuge for wild beasts, and so it remained until the Virgin deemed the time had come to restore it to human worship.

This was when Lucius, king of Britain, sent to Rome for missionaries to convert his heathen subjects to Christianity: in reply Pope Eleutherius sent two envoys, Phaganus and Deruvianus, in the year A.D. 166, to discharge this mission. The two missionaries, penetrating the forests and swamps, came to Glastonbury and found there the deserted 'church of boughs'; searching 'ancient histories', they discovered the story of its foundation by Philip's envoys, and they therefore ordained twelve new disciples, who restored the '*Vetusta Ecclesia*', and built a second church, of stone, which they dedicated to Christ and Saints Peter and Paul. In due course, having converted Britain to Christianity, Phaganus and Deruvianus died and were buried at Glastonbury, where their relics were still preserved in the thirteenth century. From this time the '*Vetusta Ecclesia*' was continuously served by a faithful community of twelve Christian hermits until A.D. 430, when St. Patrick arrived, took charge of the community and reorganized it as a monastery, with himself as its first abbot.

In a charter of foundation, which the revised version of the *De Antiquitate* cites in full, Patrick tells how, arriving at Ynys Witrin in A.D. 430, he found the twelve hermits, whom he names, and inspected their documents, from which he gives, in the charter, a *résumé* of the early history of the church and its community from its foundation by the disciples of St. Philip: the charter records that Phaganus and Deruvianus had obtained an indulgence of ten years for all pilgrims to the *Vetusta Ecclesia*, and that Patrick had secured a further twelve years from Pope Celestine (422–431) for such visitors. The charter then tells how St. Patrick, with Wellias, one of the twelve hermits, ascended the Tor, where they found the ruins of an ancient church, and in it, an ancient book which recorded the doings of Phaganus and Deruvianus, stating that it was they who had built the church on the Tor, had dedicated it to St. Michael, and had obtained for it an indulgence of thirty years for all pilgrims. After three months on the Tor, Patrick and Wellias, directed by miraculous signs, returned to the rest of the community, and decreed that henceforth two of the brethren should always reside in the restored church of St. Michael on the Tor, and Patrick chose two of his companions from Ireland to be the first to undertake this duty. Thirty days' indulgence is offered to anyone who assists in clearing the forest to make the church more accessible. For safety, Patrick says he has made two copies of this charter, one to remain in the *Vetusta Ecclesia* (St. Mary's), the other being deposited in St. Michael's on the Tor. That this charter is genuine, says the revized version of the *De Antiquitate*, is demonstrated by the antiquity of the script in which it is composed, and by 'ancient authors'. The narrative then goes on to record how Patrick, after ruling for many years as the first Abbot of Glastonbury, died and was buried in the *Vetusta Ecclesia* to the right of the altar.

Thereafter Glastonbury was visited by many Celtic pilgrims and saints from both Ireland and Wales, drawn thither by the fame of St. Patrick and the sanctity of the *Vetusta Ecclesia*: some came to pray at the shrine and then to depart, others to stay for a longer time, others again to live out their lives, to die and to be buried in so holy a place.

From Ireland came Patrick's favourite disciple St. Benignus, third bishop of Ireland, who gave up that office to succeed St. Patrick as Abbot of Glastonbury; St. Indraht, a noble Irish convert said to have been killed, with his companions, by pagan robbers living near Glastonbury; St. Bridget, who is said to have lived for several years at Beckery, an island site nearby, where she left several relics; and St. Columba, who arrived in A.D. 504 and may have died at Glastonbury, the narrative tells us. From Wales came St. Gildas, who died and was buried at Glastonbury, and St. David, who came with seven suffragan bishops to dedicate the *Vetusta Ecclesia*; but, sharply rebuked in a vision by Christ Himself, who declared that He had already dedicated the church to His Mother, David changed his intention, built and endowed another church, and went back to Wales, though later, in King Edgar's time, his remains were translated to Glastonbury. St. Paulinus, expelled from his Archbishopric of York by the heathen Penda of Mercia, covered the *Vetusta Ecclesia* with timber and with lead to preserve it from the weather. At the petition of the British Abbot Worgret in 601, an unnamed king of Devon gave further lands in 'Ynys Witrin' to the Abbey. Glastonbury presently came under the control of the West Saxons, and with charters of 670, granted by Kenwalch, and of 678, granted by Kenwine, and mentions of several grants by King Ine of Wessex, the narrative passes the point where we cease to be concerned with its details. The revised version of the *De Antiquitate* tells us that the truth of this story down to A.D. 430 is attested by St. Patrick's charter, guaranteed by its antique script, and also by 'the statements of ancient authors'. Other charters and 'old writers' testify to the later story, and one (unnamed) British historian, copies of whose book are to be found in the libraries of Bury St. Edmund's and of St.

Augustine's, Canterbury, says in his introduction that the earliest British Christians, on coming to Glastonbury, found there already in existence 'a church erected by no human agency, and dedicated, as many miracles testified to them, by Christ himself to his Mother'. It is a very circumstantial story, well supplied with corroborative detail and garnished with famous names to trick out what otherwise might have seemed a bald and unconvincing narrative of fantasy and miracle.

William of Malmesbury's original version had been very much simpler, less fanciful, more cautious. As it now stands in the second edition of his *De Gestis Regum Angliae*, it runs thus:—

'Since this is the point at which I must bring in the monastery of Glastonbury, let me trace from its very beginning the rise and progress of that church so far as I can discover it from the mass of source-material. Annals of good credit tell us that Lucius, King of the Britons, begged Pope Eleutherius (the thirteenth Pope in succession from St. Peter) to dispel the darkness of Britain by the light of Christian teaching. This was surely a most praiseworthy act of a great-minded ruler, eagerly to seek a faith of which he had hardly heard mention, at a time when it was persecuted by almost every other king and people to whom it was offered! As a result, missionaries sent by Eleutherius came to Britain, whose labours will bear fruit for evermore, even though the rust of ages has eroded their names. These men built the ancient Church of St. Mary of Glastonbury, as faithful tradition has handed the story down through decaying time. However, there are documents of no meagre credit, which have been found in certain places, saying thus: "No other hands than those of the disciples of Christ erected the church of Glastonbury". Nor is this totally irreconcilable with truth, for if the Apostle Philip did preach to the Gauls (as Freculfus says in the fourth chapter of his second book), then it is possible to believe that he broadcast the seed of the Word across the sea also. But lest I should appear to deceive the expectations of my readers with trifling fancies, let me come on to narrate facts of solid truth, leaving aside all these discrepancies'.

In an impressive passage on the awful and dread sanctity of the *Vetusta Ecclesia*, alluding to the pre-eminent fame of Glastonbury throughout the Celtic world before the English came, to the throngs of pilgrims who flocked to it, and the uncounted multitude of saints lying buried within its walls, William describes in detail two ancient and barely-decipherable sculpted and inscribed stone 'pyramids' standing between the Church and the monks' graveyard, recording the names of several princes and prelates, both British and West Saxon, who, he presumes, lie buried within or near these two ancient monuments. He tells us what he can of the great abbots, beginning with St. Patrick, who, he says, after having converted the Irish, became a monk, and later, abbot, at Glastonbury, and who, as had been revealed in a vision to one of the monks, died there in 472 and was buried to the right of the altar. William does not, however, make St. Patrick the first organizer of a monastic community at Glastonbury, but rather implies, by saying that Patrick became a monk there, that a monastery was already in existence at Glastonbury before Patrick came—a view which he had already stated in his *Vita Sancti Dunstani*. Nor does William even mention the marvellous charter of St. Patrick on which the thirteenth-century revisers based so much of their version: Wellias, the sojourn on the Tor, and the building of St. Michael's on the Tor, are also absent from William's original story. Though he recounts, with precise detail, the story of St. David's visit, and records

35

sojourns by Gildas, Benignus, Indraht and Bridget, he is much more sparing than were his revisers in claims that these saints died and were buried at Glastonbury. His subsequent story differs from that told by his revisers in ways which need not concern us here.

It will be seen that William carefully recounts what his Glastonbury hosts had told him, and what the documents which he saw purported to say; but his interpretation of the evidence is critical and detached. He lived in what has been called 'the great age of medieval forgery', when great churches, not to speak of princes, statesmen and lawyers, thought it at least their right, if not their duty, to manufacture documentary evidence so as to fill the gaps in existing documents when proof was needed to make good their claims to material possessions, rights, or even prestige. Living among men who employed itinerant professional forgers of documents, highly skilled in their art, William can hardly have been unaware of the practice of forgery or unskilled in the science of recognizing forged documents. He did not believe all that he saw or was told. They showed him the primitive little 'church of boughs', the *Vetusta Ecclesia* of wattle and daub so jealously protected through the centuries, and he readily believed that it was the oldest and the first Christian church in Britain. He reported, very perfunctorily, the Glastonbury story that it had been built by missionaries sent over from Gaul by the Apostle Philip —men who had been disciples of Christ while He lived. But he does not, however, commit himself to accepting this story. Courtesy and gratitude towards his Glastonbury hosts forbid him to say bluntly what he thinks, so he describes the documents on which this part of the story rests as 'letters of no meagre credit'—not very extravagant praise!—and he says that they have been found 'in certain places', as though to say openly that he had seen them at

36

Glastonbury might immediately arouse suspicion. As to the story itself, what he says in effect is 'If we really can believe that the Apostle Philip evangelized Gaul, then the statement that he also despatched a mission thence to Britain is not incredible'; but he carefully places the entire responsibility for the story of Philip's mission to Gaul on to the shoulders of Freculfus, an early ninth-century bishop of Lisieux, prefaces his premiss with an 'if', and observes circumspectly that, granted the dubious premiss, the conclusion is 'not utterly irreconcilable with truth'. So far he goes out of consideration for the feelings of his hosts: then his professional standards of historical criticism assert themselves, and he tactfully indicates his scepticism of this part of the Glastonbury story. The alternative version, attributing the evangelization of Britain and the building of the *Vetusta Ecclesia* at Glastonbury to unnamed envoys of Eleutherius, he states unequivocally as a matter of fact, placing it at the very beginning of his account. With his dismissal of the story of Philip's mission as 'all these discrepancies' and as 'trifling fancies', he leaves us in no doubt which version he prefers. For William of Malmesbury, the story of Glastonbury and of its *Vetusta Ecclesia* begins in the pontificate of Eleutherius, whose dates traditionally, though William does not cite them, are A.D. 174–189. He may have felt some secret qualms, even about this version, for he obviously finds it very remarkable that a British king who, he reflects, could scarcely have heard of Christianity, should nevertheless have appealed to the Pope for a Christian mission to convert his subjects at a time when Christians everywhere, nowhere more than in Rome, were being utterly ignored or fiercely persecuted by lay authorities. If so, any such doubts were too fleeting to shake his belief in this version of Glastonbury's early history, which he found completely convincing.

The thirteenth-century revisers of William's monograph were too well aware of the widespread circulation of William's story, both in the original version of the *De Antiquitate* and in the second edition of the *De Gestis Regum*, to feel able either to deny or to ignore William's preferred version. Accordingly, they boldly incorporated it in their story, naming Eleutherius' missionaries, whose names William had said were lost forever, and making them, not, as William had said, the first builders of the *Vetusta Ecclesia* of Glastonbury, but only the agents of its restoration, at the Virgin's bidding, after a long period of desertion and desolation. They discovered a rule of communal life which the two missionaries had decreed for the community of hermits which they re-established at Glastonbury; and the assertion that the relics of Phaganus and Deruvianus were still preserved at Glastonbury was presumably made to add conviction to these amendments of William's original story. True, the specific date which they provided for the mission, A.D. 166, was much too early for the traditional dates of Pope Eleutherius (174–189), but probably very few readers of the revized version of the *De Antiquitate* would be able to dispute this unlucky guess. The revisers reasserted, with far more detail than William's scanty allusion had allowed, the story of a first-century origin which William had rejected. They gave it a date, A.D. 63, which William had not mentioned, they provided an account of the mission, and of its first reception, which William had not done, and they carefully claimed for it only a very limited success, lest their story should provoke disbelief when readers were faced with the evident need for a mission to convert Britain in the time of Eleutherius, over 100 years later. For corroboration of this part of the story, they were careful to name, as the King of Britain who made the first grant to the mission, Arviragus, whom Geoffrey of Monmouth's

Glastonbury Tor

St. Joseph of Arimathea bearing the two cruets. From the east window of Langport Church

(*Photo C.U.P.*)

History of the Kings of Britain had named as the ruler of Britain at this time, making him the victor over the invading Roman armies of both Claudius and Vespasian, and the king who had compelled the mighty Emperors of Rome itself to accept him as an equal and independent ally—but how much, or, rather, how little credibility can be attached to Geoffrey as a valid witness, we shall see in due course.

They recounted the establishment of a religious community at Glastonbury as early as A.D. 63, thus establishing undisputed primacy in time for their house, and they described its early endowment by Celtic kings in remarkably Anglo-Saxon terms. They kept this primitive community in being long enough to establish its credentials, but extinguished it early enough to explain why the missionaries of Eleutherius found the site desolate. True to the rapidly-developing cult of the Virgin, a special feature of later twelfth and thirteenth-century Christianity, they placed Glastonbury from the first under the special care and affection of Christ's Mother. Most important of all for our purposes, they made St. Joseph of Arimathea the leader of the mission and the founder of Glastonbury, and they insinuated, without committing themselves to it, nor yet denying it, the idea that the *Vetusta Ecclesia* was not built by human hands at all, but by Christ himself. To vouch for these things, they offered a charter of St. Patrick, a somewhat improbable-sounding sort of document, and an unspecified British historian whose works were alleged to be available for consultation, not indeed at their own abbey, but at two great and distant houses whose libraries were presumably beyond suspicion in a matter concerning the prestige of Glastonbury. Although the citation of references had not been well-managed, as a whole this was a notable effort in the persuasive art of forgery—a reminder that the 'great age of medieval forgery' lasted much longer than is sometimes supposed.

One of the two principal characters of the Glastonbury Legends had thus appeared on the scene in the final version of the *De Antiquitate*, before 1250, though much of the picturesque detail of the present-day legend was still lacking—Wearyall Hill, the rooted staff which became the Glastonbury Thorn, and, most important of all, the Holy Grail. William of Malmesbury's silence on Joseph of Arimathea, whose name he never mentioned, even though he was fully aware of the Glastonbury claim of a first-century origin in a mission despatched by St. Philip from Gaul, suggests strongly that Joseph had been recruited into the story at some date between 1140 and 1240. Nor had William mentioned the other great Glastonbury personage, King Arthur, in connection with the Abbey or the place. This is not due to either ignorance of or disbelief in Arthur on William's part, for in the *De Gestis Regum* he refers at some length to Arthur's exploits, distinguishing, like a twelfth-century Collingwood, between the historic Arthur and the Arthur of Celtic legend, though he puts the dividing line much farther towards fable than would any historian of the Dark Ages writing to-day. The historic Arthur, the hero of sub-Roman Britain, he knows and praises: he will have none of the Arthur of Celtic legend and romance. Having written of Arthur's battles, he goes on 'This is that Arthur concerning whom the idle tales of the Britons rave wildly even to-day, a man truly worthy to be celebrated, not in the foolish dreams of deceitful fables, but in truthful history, since for a long time he sustained the declining fortunes of his country, and incited the unbroken spirit of the people to war'. But nowhere did William link Arthur's name with Glastonbury: he even says that 'the sepulchre of Arthur is nowhere known'. In the thirteenth-century version of the *De Antiquitate*, however, we read, not only that Arthur was a benefactor and patron of Glastonbury, but that his body was buried at Glastonbury, which was the same place as Avalon; whereas William had said that Arthur's burial place was 'nowhere to be seen'. Thus the thirteenth-century version of William's monograph brings into the Glastonbury story the second great figure in the Glastonbury legend, King Arthur, of whose connection with the Abbey William of Malmesbury had been totally unaware. What had made these two great changes possible?

IV

As we have seen, it was not because Arthur was unknown to Anglo-Norman writers that he did not figure in William of Malmesbury's original account of the Glastonbury Legend: it was simply that the non-Celtic world, though aware of the Celtic Arthurian stories, ignored them as uncouth, barbaric fantasies unfit to occupy the interest of civilized and cultivated men. The Arthurian Legend, therefore, had hitherto remained the exclusive property of the peoples of the 'Celtic fringe'—Wales, Cornwall, Brittany and Southern Scotland, though Anglo-Norman, French and even Italian writers were contemptuously aware of the magical tales of Arthur current in the remote north-west. The Celts had taken the dimly remembered figure of the historic Arthur—assuming, as most present-day experts in the history of sub-Roman Britain do, that there was such a figure in late fifth- or early sixth-century Britain—and had swiftly transmuted him into a legendary King of an unreal world of faery in the remote past, though still retaining some slight points of contact with both the geography and the history of late Celtic Britain. These legends were preserved in the stories of the Mabinogion and in other primitive Welsh tales which are usually grouped with the 'four branches' of the Mabinogion strictly so called.

They tell us nothing of the historic Arthur or of his wars against the encroaching Saxons, or indeed of anything which modern historians can use as direct historical evidence. Instead, these legends have done what the early French epics did with Charlemagne, save that they have carried the process of transmutation much farther into the world of unreal fantasy. Arthur is the great king, secure in age, experience, glory and authority, his past triumphs taken for granted and not even the subject of reminiscent allusion: his apotheosis is complete. His court is the centre of the whole Celtic world—no outside world is acknowledged —and it cannot be located in one fixed place (certainly not 'Camelot'). Yet it is the point of resort of all who are of noble birth or high office, and of all who seek to make their way in the world by attracting the approval of the greatest of all Celtic rulers. Arthur himself figures but rarely and exceptionally as the prime actor in these tales: it suffices that he is there and that his presence and authority provide the ethos of this vivid but unreal world. It is the young men who come to his court who are the subjects, the heroes, of these stories, though they may and do seek Arthur's decisive intervention, either in judgment or in action, when they find themselves checked by evil forces too strong for their unaided efforts, and a supreme authority must be invoked, like a *deus ex machina*. But Arthur is always there in the background, often becoming a necessary, indispensable factor in the story, providing a fixed basis of grandeur, glory, and moral assurance necessary to the existence of a stable and ordered society, even in the magic world of faery. The legends are utterly fantastic and dream-like, not of this world at all, even when they can be related to the topography of parts of Britain, as they sometimes can, or to British history (a far more dubious exercise). They deal in monsters, giants, magic, wizardry and enchantment, as well as in human qualities of courage, fortitude, loyalty and love, and despite the beauty of their fantastic imagination,

43

they often need the expert skill of the student of comparative folklore to elucidate their meaning. Their appeal to the Welsh and their other Celtic kinsmen in Brittany, Cornwall, and Southern Scotland is obvious and easy to understand, but these very qualities made the historians and writers of the rest of Western Europe impatient and contemptuous, scorning the Arthurian Legends as the worthless heritage proper only to a defeated barbaric culture.

It was probably about 1138 that Geoffrey of Monmouth changed the whole literary and historical standing of the Arthurian Legend almost overnight, by publishing his fabulous *Historia Regum Britanniae*, his *History of the Kings of Britain*, the first account in Latin of the history of the British people, and in particular of the supposed exploits of King Arthur. This is not the place to attempt any critical discussion of the identity of Geoffrey, the exact dating of his work, or the sources of his information: these are extremely complex and difficult topics over which scholars have argued long, now with the patient critical standards proper to their science, at other times with a bitter fury equalling the worst *odium theologicum*. The subject is a Serbonian bog into which even the expert ventures at his peril, while all around its edges are the bewilderments of the lunatic fringe of speculation which all such fantasies inevitably attract to themselves. Our purpose is merely to take the essential facts upon which there is little or no serious disagreement among rational scholars who stick firmly to evidence, and to use these facts in so far as they may help us to explain the development of the Glastonbury Legend in the 125 years between the date of William of Malmesbury's first edition of his *De Antiquitate* and the final version circulated by the Glastonbury monks about 1240–1250.

It is relevant to state what little we know or can safely deduce concerning Geoffrey of Monmouth himself. He was a Welshman by birth and upbringing, and still more by sentiment and patriotism, though he was certainly not a man of pure Welsh blood and culture, a man of *pura Wallia*, Welsh Wales, the regions of the north-west where Welsh princes and chieftains still held rule, and Welsh life was as yet relatively little changed by the impact of English and Norman ways. He described himself as Geoffrey 'of Monmouth', and under this name his contemporaries referred to him, so that evidently he came from the southern March of Wales, and presumably he was either born or reared in or near to Monmouth, in what was Norman March territory, not Welsh. At times he called himself 'Geoffrey Arthur': he used this name in more than one charter to which he acted as witness. Perhaps 'Arthur' was his father's name: the Welsh at this time and for centuries later used patronymics when the English were beginning to use fixed family surnames passing unchanged from father to son. But 'Arthur' was at this time by no means a common name among the Welsh, in spite of, or possibly because of the glory of that name in Celtic legend: indeed, it may be doubted if any proved instance of the use of 'Arthur' as a personal name of any Welshman has been discovered for so early a date as 1136. In Brittany, however, the name had already become fashionable—Henry II's grandson, the ill-fated heir of Constance of Brittany and of Henry's third son Geoffrey, was to be named 'Arthur' as a means of rallying Breton loyalty to the offspring of the alien Norman-Angevin stock. It has therefore been suggested that Geoffrey of Monmouth may have been of Breton descent on his father's side and of Welsh blood on his mother's; and while this possibility must remain mere conjecture, it receives some corroboration from the fact that Breton soldiers of fortune

45

had established themselves in the southern March of Wales by fighting alongside and in the service of the conquering Normans. If Geoffrey really was of mixed Breton and Welsh descent, much of his passionate British patriotism would be immediately explained. Or again, it is possible, though unlikely, that Geoffrey himself assumed the name 'Arthur' out of reverence for his chosen hero, whom he was to portray as the greatest and most glorious of all Welshmen.

His Christian name 'Geoffrey' and his place in contemporary society mark him out as one of that small but remarkably distinguished group of culturally Norman-Welsh who made such an impression on the intellectual and governmental life of twelfth-century England—men who, while remaining at heart proudly and passionately Welsh, always conscious of the differences between themselves and the typical Anglo-Normans, were yet, thanks to their half-Norman (or half-Breton) blood and their Norman speech, and to a standard clerical upbringing in the Anglo-Norman Church, or even in the schools of Paris, able to take their places in either Church or State in Norman and Angevin England. Thus they could loyally serve their French-speaking kings or the universal Catholic and Latin-speaking Church, and yet keep their essential pride in their Welshness, even though by birth, education and career, no less than by political or ecclesiastical allegiance, they were totally cut off from the narrow, intense little world of *pura Wallia* in Gwynedd or Deheubarth. Such men were Walter Map, the famous clerk, judge and scholar who served Henry II of England, and Giraldus Cambrensis, Gerald of Wales, one of the most brilliant literary and scholarly figures of late twelfth and early thirteenth century England, who, but for the implacable refusal of three successive kings, would have become the lawfully elected and consecrated Bishop of St. Davids, and conceivably the first Archbishop of Wales. Geoffrey of Monmouth was the first of these three significant Norman-Welshmen, who naturally took their places with the Norman conquerors of England and of the Marches of Wales and made their distinguished careers in this service. But we must never forget that, despite his possible Breton descent, his Norman culture and his career in the English Church, Geoffrey remained a passionate Welshman, proud of his Welshness and hotly resentful of the subordinate and despised state into which his people had fallen.

He was, it seems, a canon of the small college of secular Augustinian Canons of St. George, at Oxford, and the six genuine charters which he witnessed between 1129 and 1151 are all concerned with religious houses in or near Oxford. He described himself as 'Magister', which even at that early date should imply that he was a university graduate, presumably a Master of Arts of Paris, for the University of Oxford was still at least a generation away. In five of the six charters which Geoffrey witnessed, the name of Walter, Archdeacon of Oxford, appears either as grantor or as co-witness with Geoffrey, and as we shall see, Walter played a decisive part in Geoffrey's own account of the source from which he drew the information which he used for his great *History*. Walter was, in fact, the Provost of the College of St. George at this time, and Robert of Chesney, the grantor of the charter which Geoffrey witnessed in 1151, had been another of the canons of St. George, though in 1148 he had become Bishop of Lincoln: it was to Robert that Geoffrey dedicated his *Life of Merlin*. It is these facts that have led to the conclusion that Geoffrey himself was one of the canons of St. George at the time when both Walter the Archdeacon and Robert of Chesney were there. In 1151 Geoffrey was elected to the Bishopric of St. Asaph's, and, after taking priest's orders at Westminster in February 1152, he was consecrated Bishop at Lambeth in that same month by Archbishop Theobald. Whether he ever visited his See is doubtful, nor do we know whether he was ever able to enjoy any of its revenues, for by 1155 he was dead, and the fierce rebellion of Owen Gwynedd of North Wales against the authority of the English king and the power of the Norman lords in the northern Marches of Wales during the closing years of Stephen's ineffectual reign makes it highly unlikely that a Normanized Welshman like Geoffrey, who had sought his career in the service of the hated Norman conquerors, would ever have been received as Bishop of St. Asaph's until the Anglo-Normans regained effective control of north-east Wales. So, although in the end Geoffrey attained the ecclesiastical promotion which his published books were intended to assist, it is highly doubtful whether his episcopal rank ever brought him either effective authority or material profit.

In writing his *History*, what Geoffrey did was to provide, for the first time ever, what he claimed was a continuous history of the British people, in the form of a narrative account of the achievements of their ninety-nine kings from Brutus, the founder of the British nation, to Cadwallader, who died, Geoffrey tells us, in A.D. 689—a period of nearly 2,000 years. It is nearly all, of course, mixed fable and fantasy, though the story begins to have some slight tangential contact with historical fact when Geoffrey brings Julius Caesar's invasions of Britain into his narrative. Thereafter we increasingly recognize occasional names and incidents from genuine British history, distorted though they are almost beyond identification in the fantastic mirror of Geoffrey's story. From about A.D. 600, however, Geoffrey's 'history', though still at variance with what we know from other, and far more dependable, sources, becomes rapidly more capable of being reconciled with accepted historical fact. Actually, almost at the very end of his *History*, Geoffrey's account of the achievements of Cadwallo, whom he regards as the last of the heroic kings of the Britons, though it contains much that accords ill with the commonly accepted history of the later seventh century, might not unfairly be regarded as genuine history told from the Welsh point of view, just as the *Anglo-Saxon Chronicle* narrates these same happenings from the English standpoint.

But, apart from these last few pages, barely one-twentieth of the whole *History*, Geoffrey is not really concerned with historical fact at all, except where sheer necessity forces him to do it at least the homage of distorting it to suit his unfaltering purpose. What he is writing is an indignant and impassioned Welshman's revenge on history in general, and, in particular, on all those peoples and leaders who, over the whole course of history, had at various times harried, plundered, defeated or conquered the Britons and had torn from them all but the little-regarded mountainous western extremities of their island, and were even now seeking to bring these last refuges of a once-free people into final subjection. To adapt current critical jargon, what Geoffrey was writing might be called 'anti-history', disregarding utterly what, even in the early twelfth century was universally known and accepted historical fact unless, exceptionally, the facts of real history could, after sufficient distortion, be woven successfully into the fabric of Geoffrey's dream fantasy. He was concerned, not with historical truth or known fact, but with painting a picture of a British race and nation able to boast of an origin not a whit less ancient and noble than that of the Greeks or the Romans, nor in any way less divinely favoured than the

Jews, and, once established in Britain, invariably and crushingly victorious over all its foes, whether in self-defence or in aggression. Their leaders, according to Geoffrey, were heroes of super-human courage and prowess, skilled and cunning in all the practices of war, and able invariably to inspire the Britons to feats of heroism and unity which gave them victory even over impossible numerical odds. In short, here is the story of a nation which could never be defeated until eventually the people betrayed themselves by shameful and supine lethargy and by fratricidal strife in civil war. He was but anticipating Shakespeare's superb boast:

Come the three corners of the world in arms,
And we shall shock them: nought shall make us rue,
If [Britain] to itself do rest but true.

To this end of providing his people with a past even more glorious than that of any other known race, Geoffrey begins by telling, with a wealth of circumstantial detail, how Brutus, a mythical great-grandson of Aeneas of Troy, was born in Italy, but, having, in a hunting accident, had the misfortune to kill his own father Silvius, was exiled to Greece. Here he found the enslaved fragments of the Trojan people, suffering grievously under the tyranny of their Greek captors, and, like another Moses, Brutus united his people under his own leadership, though his methods, different by far from those of the Jewish saviour of his people, were those of a ruthlessly cunning and ferocious guerilla leader. By these means he not only restored the fighting quality of his people, but even managed, by skilful generalship and even by treachery, to capture the King of the Greeks. Brutus forced him, as the price of his liberty, not only to set the Trojans free, but to provide a great fleet of ships for their departure, to allow them to spoil the

Greeks of vast treasure, and even—a romantic touch, this, with no parallel in the sterner story of the Jewish Exodus— to carry off as Brutus' bride the Greek king's eldest daughter Ignone, a stroke which incidentally made the descendants of Brutus the heirs of the glories of both Troy and Greece alike!

Brutus now embarked on a long voyage of years of perilous adventure, seeking a permanent home for himself and his re-created people. On his way he fought with and crushed the kings and peoples of 'Africa', Spain, Aquitaine, Poitou (i.e., according to Geoffrey, the 'Pictavenses', or Picts) and Gaul. Eventually, guided by the goddess Diana, he led his people to the incomparable island of Albion, hitherto inhabited only by a handful of non-human giants, such as Gogmagog and the like. After ridding the island of these unworthy and monstrous inhabitants, Brutus peopled it with his Trojans, renaming the island 'Britain', after himself, and his followers, 'Britons'. The whole island was theirs, and they first divided it into provinces with historic names, some fanciful, some real; they began to till the ground, to exploit its natural riches; and to build towns and cities, of which the greatest was 'New Troy', Troia Nova, later corrupted to 'Trinovantum' and finally re-named 'London' by King Lud, one of Brutus' remote descendants living more than 1,000 years later as a contemporary of Julius Caesar.

From this glorious origin of the British nation Geoffrey went on to recount the generations of the house of Brutus throughout the ages, and to record the great deeds wrought by the Britons under the leadership of the more distinguished warriors of Brutus' line. Familiar legendary kings appear in the story—Hudibras (c. 874 B.C.), Leir (c. 753 B.C.), Gorboduc, and Lud—and even such historic figures as Cassivelaunus and Cymbeline (Cunobellinus); we read of Lucius, who successfully besought Pope Eleutherius to send Christian missionaries to convert his heathen subjects (*c.* A.D. 156): of the Roman Emperor Severus (A.D. 208–211) and the great Roman commander Constantius (A.D. 296–306) and his son the Emperor Constantine (306–337), of the pretender Maximianus, and of the short-lived Emperor of Britain Constantine II (early fifth century). While many, even most, of the names are legendary or invented, the historical figures often appear in recognizable if distorted form. In this long line of great leaders, the greatest of all, after Brutus himself, is Brennius, Geoffrey's second British superman. Driven from Britain in a quarrel with his elder brother Belinus, Brennius, by sheer ruthless military genius and unceasing aggression, makes himself master of the whole of Gaul. Then, reconciled with Belinus, Brennius leads joint Gallo-British invasion of Italy, expelling in his stride an army of German invaders of that country, crushing the Roman army and finally besieging and capturing Rome itself—a superb indication of the might of British arms, which had captured the master-city of the ancient world!

When Julius Caesar invaded Britain, he was, in Geoffrey's *History*, twice ignominiously defeated by the heroic Cassivellaunus and forced to take refuge in his ships and to return to Gaul. Only by a third invasion, when Cassivellaunus is betrayed by the rebellion of his nephew Androgeus, does Caesar succeed in defeating the Britons and in forcing them to pay tribute to Rome; and even then, thanks only to Androgeus' stern warning that he had helped Caesar, not in order to see Britain subjected to Roman conquest, but only to bring his uncle Cassivellaunus to reasonable terms, and that if Caesar persisted in his ambition to conquer Britain, he would find Androgeus and his powerful army at once arrayed against him.

Whereupon Caesar, not daring to tackle a united Britain for a third time, made peace with the Britons, as equal allies and trusted friends, both, after all, sprung from the same Trojan stock, which made it unthinkable that the Romans should ever treat the Britons as a defeated and conquered people.

In similar vein, when Claudius invaded Britain, Geoffrey tells us that the Romans were shamefully routed, and that it was only by a treacherous ruse employed by one of their generals (who paid with his life for the temporary success of his trickery) that Claudius and his forces avoided the same ignominious fate of expulsion from Britain which had twice humiliated the great Julius Caesar. Eventually, Claudius, by diplomacy, persuaded the dauntless and victorious British king, Arviragus, whose might the Romans dared not encounter again in an open pitched battle where no subterfuge could save them, to negotiate once more an honourable peace on terms of an equal alliance, arguing that it could be no disgrace for a people sprung from the same Trojan stock as the Romans now to accept a merely nominal Roman overlordship, seeing that Rome had now conquered all the rest of the world. On this understanding, and accepting Claudius' daughter Genvissa as his bride, Arviragus made an equal and honourable peace with Rome, and the Romans, after helping Arviragus to conquer the Orkneys and other outlying islands, withdrew from Britain and left Arviragus in complete control of the whole land. Even the future Emperor Vespasian, who later attempted to force Arviragus to do homage to the Roman Senate, was defeated and expelled from Devon by Arviragus, whom neither Roman menaces nor invasions could ever subdue.

Thus Rome never conquered Britain, and on the contrary, a British leader Brennius and his brother Belinus had captured Rome itself, while every Roman invasion of Britain had ended in crushing and humiliating defeats for the hitherto invincible legions of Rome, and a magnanimous peace granted by the victorious British king on the basis of an equal alliance with the masters of all the rest of the known world. And finally, it was yet another British hero, Constantine I, son of the great Roman general and senator Constantius and his wife Helen, daughter of King Coel (Cole) of Britain, who, after being raised to his grandfather's throne, led a great and victorious British army, in the name of Christ and of the Christian religion, to the invasion and conquest of Gaul and Italy, the defeat of every rival for the Imperial throne, and the capture of Rome itself. Thus Constantine I, King of Britain, a scion of the glorious stock of Brutus, achieved the crowning triumph and fame of enthronement as the first Christian Emperor of Rome and the ruler of the whole world. Such was Geoffrey of Monmouth's revenge on history and on the Roman conquerors of Britain.

It was all very well for Geoffrey to deal in this arbitrary fashion with the Roman period of British history: the Romans indeed 'came, saw, and conquered', and for 350 years they gave to Southern Britain a unity and a measure of ordered, civilized government such as Britain was not to enjoy again until, soon after Geoffrey's time, Henry II imposed on his English kingdom a similar degree of authority and effective rule. But, after all, by A.D. 410 Roman rule had utterly vanished from Britain and had speedily become no more than a vague memory of which the Britons themselves, a century later, retained only the most inaccurate and shadowy recollection, so that by 1135 Geoffrey's fabled *History* might well pass muster among the uncritical and credulous of his contemporaries, so far as his account of the Romano-British period was concerned. And

Glastonbury Abbey—The Lady Chapel

Glastonbury Abbey seal (14th century version)
showing the Thorn

(*Society of Antiquaries*)

The Glastonbury Pilgrimage procession

(*Photo by courtesy of Mrs. R. H. Treharne*)

as for the pre-Roman period, no one at all professed any knowledge of that, and Geoffrey's story, no matter how fantastic, had no rival history to discredit what he wrote. But when he came to the fifth, sixth and seventh centuries, his position was utterly different. The inescapable facts were that eventually the English had indisputably conquered and permanently settled the whole of what, by Geoffrey's time, was now the 250-years old Kingdom of England, and also the eastern half of Southern Scotland: that the Picts possessed the greater part of Scotland; and that the Scots, sixth-century emigrants from Northern Ireland, had first conquered western Scotland and had eventually united the whole country into a formidably compact and potentially dangerous Kingdom of Scotland, absorbing the Britons of Strathclyde in the process. As for the remaining Britons, they were now relegated to the most mountainous and least valuable parts of Wales, having lost to the Normans the more fertile plains and valleys of the east and the south-east—the Marches of Wales—and to the single county of Cornwall, by now a part of the kingdom of England for nearly three centuries. A fragment of the British people, emigrating to Armorica early in the sixth century, had gained control of that harsh moorland peninsula, and had for ever stamped their Celtic character upon it as the land of Brittany, an autonomous vassal county of the Kingdom of France. These were patent facts of twelfth-century life and politics which Geoffrey could neither ignore nor explain away: even his unbridled imagination had to allow for them in his *History*.

So Geoffrey's tale of the centuries from the final collapse of Roman authority in Britain to the end of his *History* has to be, in final effect, a story of disaster, defeat, extirpation, conquest and flight. The Picts and the Scots, despised savages though they were, harry and ravage the Britons: the

English conquer and dispossess them, either exterminating them or driving them to remote refuges in the mountains of Wales. Yet even so, it is hard to see, from reading Geoffrey's *History*, how all this came about, for although the English behave with all the savagery, cunning and treachery that Geoffrey can invent to discredit them, they are almost invariably defeated in battle whenever an heroic British king or war-leader arises to unite his people and inspire them to feats of arms. Time and time again the English are either exterminated or forced to a shameful peace: apparently they lost all the battles but won the war! The explanation is, of course, in the first place, the disunity of the British, their internecine strife of brother against brother, nephew against uncle, even son against father, and the base treachery which civil war waged in the face of a common enemy inevitably brings into play. Defeated claimants of power, or weaker contestants fearing defeat, call in the hated and abominable English to their aid, and thus eventually the heathen English gain a permanent footing, and finally master the whole of southern Britain, not by victory in open battles, but by cunning politics in exploiting the fatal divisions of the British and by sly treachery whenever opportunity serves. And even when the Britons were not at war among themselves and inviting the English barbarians to join in, there was the second great cause of defeat, the supine lethargy of a once-great people trusting in their former glory to save them from the consequences of their own inaction, and becoming ever more incapable of the unity, courage and self-sacrifice, and even of the plain hardihood in battle and of the discipline of obedience to leadership which alone would enable them to survive in times of primitive violence. It is by such shameful betrayals that Geoffrey explains the troubles of the British in face of the contemptible barbarians from

Caledonia, the Picts and the Scots, and their ultimate conquest and expulsion by the equally barbaric English.

Yet, despite the lamentable and bitter fate which, in the end, Geoffrey cannot avoid recording for the Britons, misery and shame are not the prevailing impressions left by this last portion—nearly a third of the whole book—of Geoffrey's *History*. For although the known end must close his story, in the telling of it, nevertheless, he finds heroism, greatness and triumph, the most supreme of all the achievements of the British race, to record at full length even in these fatal centuries. Great leaders and kings, all more or less directly of Brutus' royal stock, arise again and again to rally the supine and discouraged Britons to yet another superb effort of united self-defence. Again and again Picts, Scots, Angles and Saxons are defeated and crushed, even for the time being, totally exterminated, so that the reader is driven to wonder how, after all, the Britons ever were defeated and dispossessed. And now not only courage, leadership and skill save the Britons: they have magic also on their side, the magic of Merlin, the greatest of all magicians and soothsayers, if also, at times, the most obscure! Aurelius Ambrosius (the Ambrosius Aurelianus of history) and Utherpendragon in the fifth century, and Cadwallo in the seventh, continue against Picts, Scots and English the heroic and, still more, the triumphant leadership of the Britons in the old, great vein. And in between them, in the first half of the sixth century, stands the colossal figure of Geoffrey's greatest hero, Arthur of Britain, under whom the military glory and achievements of the British race reach their supreme heights.

Arthur, son of Utherpendragon, conceived by his mother with the aid of Merlin's magic, and destined by Merlin's prophecies to achieve even more than the greatest of his mighty predecessors, is the climax of Geoffrey's narrative of 2,000 years of British history. The account of his achievements occupies more than a sixth of the whole book. The narrative is thoroughly in keeping with the magical circumstances of Arthur's birth, and is just as credible. Succeeding his father Utherpendragon at the age of fifteen, Arthur at once successfully attacks the menacing Saxons, Scots and Picts, and defeats them in battle on the River Douglas, his first great victory. He then summons to his aid his kinsman, Hoel of Brittany, and in a vigorous northern campaign, winning victory after victory, he and Hoel defeat Saxons, Scots and Picts again and again, exterminating or expelling most of them from Britain, and so subjugating the remainings Scots and Picts that Hoel and he are able to embark on a tour of the beauties of Loch Lomond and of the surrounding Highlands. And this is merely a brief prelude to what is still to come—indeed, the reader senses Geoffrey's impatience to be done with the necessary but trivial story of the expulsion of the Saxons, so that he may come to the vastly more glorious episodes of Arthur's career of world-wide conquest.

Having married the peerless Guinevere and restored Britain to security and prosperity, rebuilding her wasted cities and fortresses, Arthur now embarks on a career of conquest which might have daunted Julius Caesar himself, and which only Alexander of Macedon ever exceeded. He conquers Ireland, he subjugates the Orkneys and 'Gothland' (wherever Geoffrey imagined that country to be), Norway and Denmark, setting his captains and kinsmen to rule these conquered lands. Gaul next falls before his invincible armies, including Poitou and Aquitaine, the Roman legions proving powerless to withstand him. Once more his faithful captains are rewarded with rich duchies and counties, such as Normandy and Aquitaine. Arthur pauses briefly in his career of conquest to return to Britain, where he holds a 'plenary court' at the ancient Roman legionary fortress of Caerleon-on-Usk, attended by all the vassal kings, dukes and counts of his vast European Empire. Now he receives an insolent summons to come to Rome to stand trial before the Senate for his crimes of rebellion and aggression against the Roman Republic, which he answers by invading Gaul yet again with an army of nearly 200,000 men, drawn from all parts of his wide dominions. He so chastizes the presumptuous but ineffective Roman armies that, after a winter in Gaul, he is ready to set out to capture Rome itself, and such is the certainty of his victory that the Romans themselves quail at his approach, knowing that nothing can now save them from the vengeance and justice of Arthur and his Britons.

But the final reckoning was never made: in the face of what twelfth-century men knew of the fate of Rome in the fifth and sixth centuries, not even Geoffrey of Monmouth dared to substitute Arthur of Britain for Alaric the Visigoth or the Vandal Gaiseric as captor of Rome in a known historical context. In any case, surely Arthur had by now done all that was needed to ensure the lasting glory of British arms; while on the other hand something had to be done to explain why, long before A.D. 600, most of Britain had passed irrevocably into English hands. So Geoffrey advances his favourite reason for the ultimate defeat of the Britons—rebellion, civil war, and treachery.

At the moment when Arthur's crowning triumph, the capture of Rome itself, was within his grasp, news came that his nephew Mordred, Duke of Cornwall, had seduced Queen Guinevere and had started a dangerous rebellion to dethrone his uncle, calling in the Saxons once more to aid him in his evil design. Surprisingly, for we are given no reason, Mordred found much support, and Arthur had to abandon all thought of seizing Rome, and instead he hastened back to Britain. In a fiercely-fought campaign he won a succession of battles against Mordred and forced him back to his base in Cornwall. But in the final battle on the River Camlan, where Mordred was justly slain, Arthur himself received a fatal wound for which there was no earthly cure. At this last tragic moment, the supernatural world intervened to save Arthur from death and to leave to the Britons the future hope that one day he would return to lead them yet again to the fulfilment of their destined supremacy. For Arthur did not die by the Camlan, as any other mortal king would have died: he 'was carried away to the Isle of Avalon for the healing of his wounds'—by what agency Geoffrey does not tell us. But among the Britons everywhere, in Cornwall, Brittany and even in Scotland, no less than in Wales itself, his memory remained imperishable, and with it the undying hope, even the certainty, that Arthur was not dead, but lay sleeping under a magic spell until the time should come when, according to Merlin's cloudy prophecy, he would return to lead his people to their freedom and to the final triumphant consummation of their mighty destiny.

Such then, in salient outline, is the fabulous *History of the Kings of Britain* of Geoffrey of Monmouth, which was to prove one of the most influential books of the Middle Ages, not only in Britain, but throughout Western Europe, including Germany. That it was fable and legend, not history, is self-evident, even though from time to time it touched, briefly and tangentially, the lines of history as known to twelfth-century chroniclers and historians—and we must remember that the twelfth century was unquestionably the greatest age of medieval historical scholarship in England. It is doubtful whether any similar concoction of nonsense and baseless imagination has ever been offered to the educated world as the seriously-intended history of a nation, either before or since Geoffrey's time. How, then, did he come by the 'facts', the 'events' and the persons whom he wove into this astonishing romance? What, other than his own unrestrained imagination, were the sources on which he drew?

We can show, from closely parallel passages, that he used Bede's *Ecclesiastical History of the English People* for the topographical description of Britain with which Geoffrey prefaced his *History*; for his account of the Christian mission which Pope Eleutherius, at the request of King Lucius, sent to Britain, though Geoffrey adds important and independent detail to Bede's story, and gives much too early a date for this momentous conversion; and for a large number of the later happenings which Geoffrey narrates in his account of the wars between the Britons and the English, especially in the late sixth and the seventh centuries, when he could not conceivably have ignored Bede's quiet but masterly historical scholarship. We can also identify matter taken from Gildas' sixth-century *De excidio Britanniae*, especially Gildas' confused account of the Roman 'withdrawal' from Britain and his famous story of the appeals to the Emperor Honorius and to the Roman commander-in-chief Agitius for aid against the encroaching barbarians, as well as some other less important passages. But, beyond question, of all the works surviving to us today from the Dark Age period of British history, it was from that extraordinary compilation, probably made about A.D. 800, usually known as the *Historia Brittonum* of Nennius, that Geoffrey drew most heavily. Nor was this merely for the period after the end of Roman rule in Britain: it is astonishing and sobering to see how much of Geoffrey's story of the earlier periods of British history is taken, in essential ideas at least, from Nennius' hotch-potch of fantasy seasoned with a little, obscurely remembered fact. It

61

was in Nennius that Geoffrey found the bare bones (though no more) of the story of Brutus and of the Trojan origin of the British race, as well as of their long wanderings before they came to Britain. The first coming of the Scots to Ireland, with the compassionate and generous permission of the Britons; the account of the placing of sharpened wooden stakes, shod with lead and iron, in the bed of the Thames to prevent Julius Caesar's ships from sailing up the river to attack London; and many other incidental happenings, before ever Geoffrey comes to the beginning of the long struggles of the Britons and the English, can all be traced from Geoffrey's *History*, back to Nennius—unless both authors were drawing on some common original now lost to us, as one recent scholar has argued. From that point onwards, starting with his highly circumstancial and romantic account of Vortigern and of his bringing of the first Saxon mercenaries, under Hengist and Horsa, into Britain, and of all the catastrophies that issued from this fatal error, Nennius becomes and remains the most important of Geoffrey's sources which we can identify today. Scholars expert in Geoffrey's text and in the surviving literature of the Dark Ages of British history tell us that he also used the Latin *Annales Cambriae*, some Welsh royal genealogies, the *Life of St. David* and other lives of sixth-century Celtic saints, and that he was very closely acquainted with Welsh folk-lore, especially with the legends of the *Mabinogion* and its associated stories. All of this use of known source-material, whether reliable or not, adds up to a quite considerable body of derived information which Geoffrey found in the works of earlier writers.

Even so, the identifiable borrowings, apart from a few limited passages copied almost as they stand from Gildas and from Bede, are the merest bare bones of Geoffrey's narrative, providing only the most skeletal material for isolated portions, however important, of the long-sustained and continuous *History* which Geoffrey wrote. How did he make these dry bones live? By what breath of inspiration did he contrive the articulation of these disjointed and scattered remains, bringing bone to bone, clothing them with flesh, and making the whole structure come to life, as undoubtedly he did? Where did he find the wealth of circumstantial and stirring detail which he uses to animate and vivify those bare statements which we can show he drew from earlier writers, and whence came the long, sustained passages of narrative for which, so far as we know, no known earlier source existed? It is tempting to say simply that he invented it all himself, both the totally new material which forms by far the greater part of his *History*, and the detail with which he clothes the meagre extracts which he took from identifiable sources. But, likely though this explanation seems, especially as Geoffrey was a Celt and wrote as a Celt, with all the boundless fertility of Celtic imagination at his disposal, we dare not assert this view without qualification.

Geoffrey himself knew that he would be accused at least of unbridled invention, if not of down-right lying, and he took care to provide himself with an authority which none of his critics would be able to check—a not uncommon device of medieval authors eager to tell a new tale and to have it accepted as truth, escaping the charge of mere invention. He said, more than once, that he obtained the facts of his *History* from 'a certain very ancient book written in the British tongue',* which had been given to him by his friend Walter, Archdeacon of Oxford, 'a man . . . well-informed about the history of foreign countries' and 'most learned in all branches of history',* who, as we have seen,

---

* The four quotations in this paragraph all come from Lewis Thorpe's translation of *Geoffrey of Monmouth's History of the Kings of Britain*, pp. 51, 258.

was Provost of the Augustinian College of St. George where Geoffrey himself was one of the canons. Geoffrey tells us that, at Walter's request, he has 'taken the trouble to translate this book into Latin', and he implies that he has kept pretty closely to the original sense of the wording, for he says, 'I have been content with my own expressions and my own homely style, and I have gathered no gaudy flowers of speech in other men's gardens: for, if I had adorned my page with highly-flown rhetorical figures, I should have wearied my readers, who would have been forced to spend more time in discovering the meaning of my words than in following the story.'

It would be very easy to dismiss 'the very ancient book written in the Welsh tongue' as a mere literary device of Geoffrey's to avoid the imputation of wholesale invention: but to do so is to risk being proved wrong at some future date by the discovery of a lost original or by its convincing reconstruction by modern critical scholarship. Geoffrey indeed tells us no more about this book—who wrote it, when it was written, how it came into Walter's possession: but then, assuming for a moment that the book really existed, Geoffrey himself may not have known the answers to these very obvious modern questions. The book has never subsequently been identified, either at the time when Geoffrey wrote or since, but even that is no conclusive proof that the book existed only in Geoffrey's lively imagination, for many other medieval manuscripts, known to have existed once, have totally disappeared, and yet scholars to-day are able to reconstruct their contents in detail, and sometimes even their probable wording, by careful study of surviving works which drew upon the lost archetypes. A few modern scholars have in fact claimed to be able to discern 'the very ancient book', in outline at least, by comparing Geoffrey's *History* with Nennius and the other early Welsh chronicles which have survived to our own time, and while these claims seem very unconvincing, we dare not dismiss summarily Geoffrey's Welsh original as a mere fiction to give authority to the work of Geoffrey's audacious imagination. Yet, until we are given better evidence to the contrary, most historians will probably continue to believe that, when all allowance has been made for Geoffrey's proved drawings upon known and identifiable surviving sources, Geoffrey himself was the original source of by far the greatest part of his *History of the Kings of Britain*.

It is instructive to realize that Geoffrey used established historical sources, such as Bede, only where they would help and not hinder his main thesis, and that he carefully avoided using the great universal histories and the histories of Greece, Rome, and Gaul. These must have been well-known to him, early product of the twelfth-century Renaissance as he undoubtedly was, for all the great chroniclers of this age of great historical writers used these famous works to provide the framework of ancient and early medieval history before they came to their own original accounts of contemporary events. It is true that Geoffrey quotes from Cicero, Virgil, Juvenal, Lucan and Apuleius, none of them historians, but all affording evidence of Geoffrey's classical learning. He can even be shown to have made very sparing use of the historians Livy and Orosius, carefully selecting a very few passages from them which would not contradict his fantastic account of Ancient history. But he carefully avoided using either of them in a general way, nor did he use any of the other great Greek, Roman and early medieval writers on universal history, such as Polybius, Eusebius or Rabanus Maurus, nor did he use the more limited but authoritative writings of Julius Caesar, Gregory of Tours, Freculfus and many others who must have been known to him. He did not dare to use them, for they would immediately have contradicted virtually everything he had to say about the exploits of the Britons before the coming of the English, and they would thus have destroyed his story root and branch. It is no less significant that he chose to end his *History* with the death of Cadwallader in A.D. 689, declaring that he leaves 'to my contemporary Caradoc of Llancarfan the task of describing the kings who succeeded from that moment onwards in Wales'. He had found it difficult enough to square his narrative of the last century of the *History* with historical fact known to all educated men of his time: to have taken his fantasy still farther into the known historical period would have been impossible.

He had indeed the colossal impudence to offer, as a specious corroboration of his story, dating equations between his *History of the Britons* and events in the Biblical and the Classical worlds. Thus, Brutus is the great-grandson of Aeneas, and his reign in Britain coincided with the judgeship of Eli among the Jews: Ebraucus, King of Britain and founder of York (Eburacum), was the contemporary of King David: Hudibras and Bladud are contemporary with Elijah and Ahab: Leir's rule in Britain coincides with the foundation of Rome by Romulus and Remus—a nice touch this, showing Britain to have been founded as a kingdom four centuries before the foundation of the City of Rome! There are many other such cross-references which could be cited in addition. *C'est magnifique, mais ce n'est pas l'histoire*: none of this can cover the fact that although here and there his story can briefly be related to known history, however distorted the contact, it is almost entirely a superbly and shamelessly audacious work of fiction, however much of it Geoffrey drew from earlier writings, and however much he himself invented.

V

THIS ACCOUNT OF the contents and nature of Geoffrey of Monmouth's *History of the Kings of Britain* may at first sight seem irrelevant to our discussion of the Glastonbury Legends, for Glastonbury is never once mentioned by Geoffrey in the whole of his long account of British history, although long before the end of his story, and probably even as early as the dates which he attributes to King Arthur, Glastonbury had already become one of the most important Christian shrines in Celtic Britain. Yet, despite Geoffrey's silence about Glastonbury, it still remains true that without Geoffrey's fabulous History, the Glastonbury Legends could never have come into existence in the form in which we have them to-day, or even as the revised version of the *De Antiquitate* gave them about 1250. The explanation of this apparent discrepancy lies in what became of Geoffrey's story, both as history and as fiction, in the hundred years after its publication, for those years saw amazing developments in the story which Geoffrey had told. These changes must be understood if the difference between William of Malmesbury's original account of Glastonbury's early history and the final, mid-thirteenth century revision of it is to be explained, and it is for this reason that we have had to examine in some detail Geoffrey's *History* as he himself wrote it.

It will readily be seen how little of the matter of the developed form of the Glastonbury Legends Geoffrey's

History itself can provide. All that it gives is the mere germ of the Arthurian side of the Legends, the figure of Arthur himself, conceived as the greatest, the most heroic and the most victorious of British kings, with his peerless queen, Guinevere, and his supernatural passing, by which he was 'borne away to the Isle of Avalon for the healing of his wounds'. Geoffrey never identifies 'Avalon' with Glastonbury or with any other actual place: indeed, it is most improbable that he had any idea of equating 'Avalon' with any real place, in Britain or elsewhere. Magic has already entered powerfully into Geoffrey's *History* with the birth of Arthur, and at his passing magic intervenes no less decisively again, for though fatally wounded, he does not die, but is 'borne away to Avalon for the healing of his wounds' by an unnamed but obviously supernatural agency. And this end to Arthur's glorious career was necessary to Geoffrey's story: Arthur cannot die, for he is destined to re-appear at some unspecified but remote time, to lead his people to victory and freedom once more. The Isle of Avalon is therefore no more a real place in British topography than is Arthur's passing a real event in British history. 'Insula Avallonia'—'Ynys Afallon' in Welsh: what is it but 'the Isle of Apples', some mystic faery island far out in the Western Ocean, the Celtic equivalent of the Greek Hesperides, which likewise were 'Apple Islands', though for the Greeks those magic apples were of gold? Geoffrey of Monmouth never intended, and could not have intended, to identify Avalon with any real place whatsoever, let alone with Glastonbury, which he never once mentions.

Nor does he ever allude in his *History* to the first-century conversion of the British to Christianity, to St. Joseph of Arimathea, the bringing of the Holy Grail, the rooting of St. Joseph's staff and its miraculous flowering as the

Glastonbury Thorn, nor to any other part of the religious side of the Glastonbury Legends. The entire concept of the legend of the Holy Grail and of its place in popular religion and chivalric romance was as yet unborn, and so could have no place in Geoffrey's *History*. In fact, it is not unfair to say that Geoffrey's *History*, like the Norman barons and knights whom he took as his models in depicting warriors and warfare, was hardly even nominally Christian and civilized. It is quite true that he records the story of the conversion of Britain to Christianity in the second century, and that, for him, the Britons are thenceforth a Christian people ruled by Christian kings. He has three Archbishops at the head of the British Church—London, York, and Caerleon, but it is the Archbishop of Caerleon whom he styles Primate of Britain and Legate of the Papal See, and whom he therefore always casts for the role of the religious and moral spokesman of the kingdom in times of stress or crisis. Geoffrey names several bishops up and down the land, having their Sees in various Roman cantonal capitals, by the time of the persecution of Christians by the Emperor Diocletian, and he notes the traditional stories of the first Christian martyrs in Britain, St. Julian and St. Aaron at Caerleon, and St. Alban at Verulamium. He writes with pride of the triumph of the British-born and Brutus-descended Constantine as the first Christian Emperor. He suggests vaguely the idea of a 'Holy War' of the Christian Britons against the heathen Saxons, and he makes Arthur and his men fight under the sign of the Blessed Virgin after stirring Christian exhortations from the Archbishop of Caerleon. Thus put together, these instances of Christianity in Britain may seem to constitute an important Christian element in Geoffrey's *History*: but individually they read as incongruous trappings superficially imposed on an essentially savage and pagan story. In fact, the *History of the*

Britons is not at any point a Christian book in spirit or feeling: from Brutus to Cadwallo, not even excepting the heroic Arthur himself, the Kings of Britain fight as pagans fought, with a lust for battle and a savage exultation in slaughter. Whether in defence or in attack, they fight to exterminate their foes and to seize all the land and plunder they can take—the mere existence of a neighbouring people suffices to justify a ferocious war of conquest against them. The conception, generally accepted in Europe by the middle of the thirteenth century, that war between rulers and states is so harmful and wrong that it requires strong moral, or at least legal, justification, finds no place in the ethos of Geoffrey's *History*, which regards war as the natural state of relations between rulers, and victory as sufficient justification. Similarly the ideals of medieval chivalry, in their fully-developed forms, are in Geoffrey's *History* represented only by courage, prowess in battle, and loyalty to one's leader: of the nobler, semi-religious and idealistic side of the chivalric code Geoffrey's warriors show no trace. The reason for these facts is simple enough: Geoffrey wrote of kings, princes, nobles and warriors as they were at the time of his writing, when as yet the development of the chivalric ideal had not begun, and the idea of peaceful relations between neighbouring states and rulers was little more than a remote vision as yet seen only by churchmen. So Geoffrey's *History* describes a world still essentially pagan, ferocious and unbridled, with Christianity worn as an incongruous and ineffective trimming, not yet an essential part of the code of behaviour of kings and warriors, whether in war or in peace.

And so, as yet, there was no room in Geoffrey's *History* for the story of St. Joseph or for the Holy Grail. The very concept of the Holy Grail and of the quest of King Arthur's knights of the Round Table could not take shape until the half-barbaric and purely military ideal of knighthood which characterized, not only Anglo-Norman, but all West European noble society until after the middle of the twelfth century, had evolved into the far more sophisticated and civilized ideal of chivalry which, with all its faults, still constituted one of the great advances of medieval civilization. When Geoffrey of Monmouth wrote, that turning-point was still some forty or fifty years ahead, and therefore his *History* could not provide the model for the King Arthur of the Glastonbury Legends, still less the story of St. Joseph and the Holy Grail. The revised version of William of Malmesbury's *De Antiquitate* could not have been written from Geoffrey's *History* alone. Yet, even so, Geoffrey had provided the germ of the Arthurian Legend which the later Glastonbury revisers were to appropriate for the glorification of their ancient Abbey. He had presented Arthur as the great and victorious king of peerless valour, might and achievement: he had armed him with his wonderful sword Caliburn (Excalibur), 'forged in the Isle of Avalon', his shield Pridwen, 'on which there was painted a likeness of the Blessed Mary, Mother of God', his spear 'called Ron, . . . long, broad in the blade and thirsty for slaughter', his golden helmet bearing a crest 'carved in the shape of a dragon', while the standard under which he fought was likewise fashioned 'in the form of a flying dragon'. His queen Guinevere, descended from a noble Roman family, 'was the most beautiful woman in the entire island'. King Arthur held at Caerleon, for all his nobles and vassals, 'a plenary court' which, as Geoffrey described it in detail, undoubtedly inspired the later accounts of Arthur's permanent court held at Camelot in the developed Arthurian legend. But Geoffrey did not give him an organized Round Table of knights admitted by King Arthur to formal membership of this *élite* of chivalry, though

71

the germ of the legendary idea can be found in the brief passage in which Geoffrey told of the many brave and renowned knights who came to serve Arthur as their personal lord at the height of his power. 'Arthur then began to increase his personal entourage by inviting very distinguished men from far-distant kingdoms to join it. In this way he developed such a code of courtliness in his household that he inspired peoples living far away to imitate him. The result was that even the man of noblest birth, once he was roused to rivalry, thought nothing at all of himself unless he wore his arms and dressed in the same way as Arthur's knights. At last the fame of Arthur's generosity and bravery spread to the very ends of the earth'.* In the *History* we read little of these knights as individuals, but still Geoffrey tells us that Sir Bedevere was Arthur's cup-bearer and Sir Kay his seneschal, and that Arthur's nephew, Sir Gawain, was also a leader of this carefully chosen band of warriors. But of the other famous knights of the Round Table in the developed form of the legend—Sir Lancelot, Sir Galahad, Sir Tristram, Sir Perceval and the rest, and of King Mark and of Iseult, Geoffrey tells us nothing, though of course he gives us the tragic story of Guinevere's seduction by Mordred, of Mordred's rebellion, of Arthur's last but fatal victory by the River Camlan, and of his supernatural passing to the magical Isle of Avalon.

To sum up, we can say that, by relating his marvellous account of Arthur, Geoffrey of Monmouth had, in his *History of the Kings of Britain*, brought the hitherto disregarded Celtic legend of Arthur on to the very centre of the stage of West European literature, since the story he had to tell was in itself powerfully striking and Geoffrey had told it, for those who could read his Latin, in a most readable

* Lewis Thorpe, *op. cit.*, p. 222.

fashion, exactly devised to suit the tastes and stir the longings of both knightly and clerkly society in Geoffrey's own day. He had even provided some of the essential features of the Arthurian Legend as it was to develop over the next hundred years, though he had not himself done nearly enough to make it possible for the Arthurian Legend to become identified with Glastonbury in the way in which William of Malmesbury's revisers were to appropriate King Arthur before the middle of the thirteenth century. Geoffrey's *History* made King Arthur the centre of the greatest of all the romantic cycles of medieval Europe, but it was the development of the Arthurian legend in the fifty years after Geoffrey's book that explains the appropriation of the legend by the Glastonbury monks. What made the Glastonbury Legends possible, in the form in which we now have them, was the immediate and sweeping success of Geoffrey's *History* in the fifty years following its publication—a double success, since the *History* immediately established itself as the generally accepted historical account of the origin and early history of the British nation, and at the same time it was accepted as the core of a rapidly growing cycle of romantic fiction quite unrelated to time, place or fact. We need to understand both aspects of this double success of Geoffrey's fabulous *History* if we are to understand the origins of the Glastonbury Legends.

When he wrote his book, Geoffrey knew well that it would not pass muster with the scholarly historians of his own day and of later ages, and he had therefore done all he could to forestall and to discredit in advance the criticisms which he himself anticipated. It was for this reason that he had deliberately cut short his *History* with the death of Cadwallader (A.D. 689), to avoid bringing his fantastic story on to historical ground where it could and would

73

immediately be challenged by established historical fact derived from other sources. This is why he declared that he would leave the later history of his people to Caradoc of Llancarfan, (who, so far as we know, did not write any such historical account of the Welsh people or princes). In the same passage Geoffrey went on to say 'The kings of the Saxons I leave to William of Malmesbury and Henry of Huntingdon. I recommend them to say nothing at all about the kings of the Britons, since they have not in their possession the book in the British language which Walter, Archdeacon of Oxford, brought from Wales. It is this book which I have been at such pains to translate thus into Latin, for it was composed very accurately about the deeds of these princes and to their honour'.* In these words he warns know contemporary historians, and, by implication, future writers, not to trespass on his special field, whether by competition or by criticism, because, being ignorant of the Welsh tongue, they cannot check the source which he himself claims to have translated, and the accuracy of which he guarantees. No one who cannot read Welsh and who has not seen Archdeacon Walter's ancient book in the Welsh tongue, he claims, has any right to criticize the *History of the Kings of Britain*.

What either William of Malmesbury or Henry of Huntingdon thought of Geoffrey's *History* we do not know, though we can guess William's probable opinion from his scornful rejection of 'the idle ravings of the Britons' about their legendary Arthur, as contrasted with the Arthur of sixth-century historical fact. But the criticisms which Geoffrey had anticipated and which he had done his best to discredit in advance came soon enough, and Geoffrey may even have read the first expression of them shortly before he died. About 1151, Alfred (Alured) of Beverley, writing

* Lewis Thorpe, *op. cit.* p. 284, n.l.

74

a popular history now known as the *Aluredi Beverlacensis Annales*, began his chronicle with a summary version of Geoffrey's *History* because he wanted it to be true, he accepted it, and he wished to make it generally known to his countrymen. Alfred was neither a great nor a critical historian, but even so he was forced, in all honesty, to ask some very pertinent questions, little as he wished to shake the faith of his readers in Geoffrey's enthralling story. His great difficulty was the perplexing thought that none of the historians of the rest of the world appeared to have even the slightest knowledge of the wonderful succession of the mighty Kings of Britain or of the glorious achievements of the British people covering a period of more than 2,000 years, a history longer and more glorious than that of Rome itself. More particularly, Alfred was puzzled to understand how, in the sixth century A.D., Arthur could have conquered the whole of northern and western Europe, and crushed the military power of Rome itself in Gaul, without any writer among the Romans, the Greeks and the Franks leaving any hint of these stupendous happenings. Alfred asked these questions apologetically and with no desire to discredit Geoffrey's story, but they were to remain, of course, the unsurmountable stumbling blocks for every serious historian in subsequent centuries who sought to find any solid foundation of historical fact in Geoffrey's unique concoction.

Later critics were far less favourable, and none expressed his disbelief more vigorously than William of Newburgh, who, writing at the end of the twelfth century, all but identified Geoffrey of Monmouth with 'the Father of Lies' himself, and plainly so thought of him. William's outburst was all the more significant because, having set himself to write a *Historia Rerum Anglicanum* for the years 1066–1198 only, he nevertheless felt it his duty as a scholar and a historian to go far out of his way by writing an indignant preface attacking Geoffrey's work root and branch, even though a gap of four centuries lay between the end of Geoffrey's story and the beginning of his own. Geoffrey, William said, had 'cloaked fables about Arthur under the honest name of History'. He attacked the Arthurian portion of the *History* both in detail and in general principle, scoffing, for instance, at Geoffrey's tale of Arthur's miraculous victory over the terrible giant of Mt. St. Michel, and ridiculing the idea that a man whose name is never once mentioned in the chronicles and histories of neighbouring nations should have conquered the whole of Gaul in one short campaign, whereas Julius Caesar had found ten years of strenuous fighting and marching necessary for the same task. He refused to believe that a warrior whose conquests were equalled only by those of Alexander should remain utterly unknown to historians other than those of his own people. He contrasted what Geoffrey had to say about the organized Christian Church in Britain, with its three Archbishops of Caerleon, London and York and with the Archbishop of Caerleon acting as primate of Britain and Papal Legate, with what Bede had to say about the early church in Britain and what was known on the subject from other sources for early church history in the island— though here modern scholars might well say that William was attacking on very uncertain ground. William contrasted the known facts of the Anglo-Saxon conquest and settlement of England with Geoffrey's utterly discrepant account of the wars of the Britons and the English. In short, he delivered what Sir Thomas Kendrick has called 'a broadside of courageous and devastating criticism' against Geoffrey's lately-launched fabulous *History*, and 'its echoes went rumbling loudly down the ages and even disturbed antiquaries of the seventeenth and eighteenth centures'.* Scarcely any century failed to produce its disbelievers in Geoffrey's *History* until his fables were finally discarded as serious history some six hundred years after Geoffrey had started them on their astonishing career. Even Gerald of Wales, who might have been expected to be enthusiastic for his compatriot's brilliant rehabilitation of the British people and their history, was in fact too good a scholar to think well of Geoffrey's book. Although Gerald seems to have accepted the story of Brutus and the Trojan origin of the British people—which, it will be remembered, was not Geoffrey's own invention—and several other portions of the *History*, he made his general opinion of the book quite clear by telling the story of the devils who fled from the body of a man possessed when the Gospel of St. John was placed on his breast, but who returned in greater force than ever when a copy of Geoffrey's *History* was substituted for the sacred book. Gerald lets it be seen fairly plainly that he thought the *Historia Regum Britanniae* the product of Geoffrey's fertile and unbridled imagination.

But though Geoffrey's *History* scarcely at any time lacked its outspoken critics, their denunciations had, for centuries, no effect on the success of his famous work. The general public always prefers its history coloured with sensation, excitement and dramatic incident, and the more scholarly and sound the critic, the less will he be heard or credited by the general reader. Geoffrey's *History of the Kings of Britain* became a 'best-seller' almost overnight—possibly the most successful of all medieval books if we judge by its acceptance and the later developments based upon it, and there were powerful reasons for this astonishing success of a work of mere fiction masquerading as true history. In the first place, by the standards of the twelfth century and

* Sir Thomas Kendrick, *British Antiquity*, p. 13.

of the reading public at which Geoffrey had aimed, the
book was extraordinarily well-written and readable, and
it suited exactly the taste of the age, scholarly critics apart.
Whether by natural aptitude or by deliberate literary device, Geoffrey had varied most skilfully the pace and the
scale of his narrative, now taking in one broad sweep a
whole succession of reigns, now offering, to readers who
were all trained warriors by calling, the keen excitement
and the thrills of a carefully detailed account of a whole
campaign, or a close tactical description of a decisive
battle, with precise figures of the numbers engaged, clear
statements of the disposition of the opposing forces under
the various divisional commanders, and elaborate explana-
tions of the battle-plans, at least of the ever-victorious
British armies. There were enthralling stories of cunning
tactical strategems, ambushes and daring surprises, of
fiercely-waged hand-to-hand combats between the opposing champions, and rousingly eloquent set orations devised
to set mens' hearts aflame with the lust of battle and the
hope of glory. He even occasionally interpolated descrip-
tions of natural scenery, or cunningly introduced into a
swiftly-moving account of a battle or of a single combat
some vivid phrase which would make the very scene of the
struggle seem to participate in the ferocity of the warring
combatants. It was exactly suited to the thoughts and feelings of the fierce warrior-aristocracy of knights and nobles
at whose tastes it aimed, quickening simultaneously their
professional skill as soldiers and commanders, and their
individual, primitive battle-lust.

But, important for the success of his *History* as was Geoffrey's style, his matter, the 'factual' information which he
offered and the single constant theme running all through
it, counted for far more in the reception given to Geoffrey's
extraordinary book. For the first time readers were offered

the story of two thousand wonderful years of British history, nearly all of which had never previously been so much as suspected by anyone save a handful of isolated Celtic story-tellers to whom no-one outside Wales and Brittany had ever paid the slightest attention, unless to scoff at their 'wild tales'. And what a glorious and marvellous story it was that Geoffrey told, taking the history of the British people back to a point at least five hundred years before the very foundation of Rome, and rivalling the histories of the Greeks and of the Jews in its backward reach into the remotest antiquity! A story of great feats of arms, of mighty heroes and of a great people whose triumphs overtopped those of Rome and of Alexander of Macedon—well indeed might William of Newburgh exclaim that Geoffrey 'had made the little finger of his Arthur stouter than the back of Alexander the Great'! It was the history of the greatest of all the peoples in the world, if only Geoffrey's readers were willing to accept it.

Geoffrey's readers were, in fact, more than willing—they were eager to believe the story Geoffrey gave them. It mattered nothing that Geoffrey had written to rehabilitate the glory of the Britons, now represented by their modern descendants, the Welsh and the Bretons: his story was not even for a few years allowed to remain the consoling treasure of Bretons and Welshmen only, but was at once appropriated by the Norman and Angevin conquerors of England, and even, before long, by the English themselves, the execrated villains of the last sections of Geoffrey's book, who now took possession of the newly-revealed British past as if it were their own early history. Just as the Norman conquerors and their Angevin successors had taken over the English kingdom with all of its developed administrative and legal system and its well-established agrarian economy, as theirs by right of conquest and succession, and just as

79

the English had themselves appropriated the lands of the British people, so now, in the second half of the twelfth century, Angevin, Norman and English alike took over Geoffrey's *History of the Kings of Britain* and made it their own, for it gave them a pride of origin, of history and of past greatness which seemed to justify and to adorn the glory and the power of the kingdom of England under its new and ambitious Angevin dynasty. Even for the Duchy of Normandy and the County of Anjou, as distinct from the Kingdom of England, Geoffrey's *History* provided a glorious origin, since both of these principalities, Geoffrey said, were created by Arthur during his conquest of Gaul and were bestowed upon two of his greatest nobles as rewards for their parts in the conquest. Altogether, it is not too much to say that by A.D. 1200 Geoffrey's 'fabulous *History*' had proved to be even more of an inspiration to the ruling class in England than to the Welsh for whose pride and consolation it had been written.

For the monastic chroniclers in England it had the special value of enabling them to fill in some thirteen hundred years of British history before the Roman Conquest of Britain, where hitherto there had been only an utter blank, and moreover to do this to the resounding glory of the kingdom and the nation—of course on the unargued assumption that the Kingdom of England had inherited all the glory of the hundred Kings of Britain. Scholarly historians like William of Newburgh might denounce Geoffrey's *History* as a 'tissue of impudent and shameless lies', but they were but a tiny minority, and the average monastic chronicler was quite uncritical, wholly credulous, and eager to believe a book which offered him such unique riches. From the time of Alfred of Beverley onwards, most of the English chroniclers, including the lay writers of the later middle ages, summarized Geoffrey's *History* if they wished to include in their designs any account of British history before the Anglo-Saxon Conquest. Some of them took all that Geoffrey offered them, without exercising any criticism in their selections and paraphrases: others tacitly omitted those parts of Geoffrey's story which were contradicted by established and accepted history based upon other and better sources. So general was this acceptance of Geoffrey's account that before long 'the Brutus', or, more usually, 'the Brut', had become the shorthand title used by English writers for any account of early British history based, necessarily, on Geoffrey of Monmouth, while in Wales 'Brut' became the regular word for any kind of national chronicle—e.g. 'Brut y Twysogion' = The Chronicle of the Princes. And so, though each succeeding century produced its occasional critics, Geoffrey's 'fabled history' won general acceptance throughout England as being the true story of the origin and early history of the British people, and English and Norman writers alike adopted it as their own. Not until early in the sixteenth century, Polydore Vergil published his root and branch attack on 'the Brut' did belief in it begin to waver, and even then it became a matter of patriotic, and, after the Reformation, of religious duty to denounce and refute the critics of the Brut. Another two centuries or more had to pass before Geoffrey of Monmouth's *Historia Regum Britanniae* was finally consigned to the category to which it rightly belongs —an audaciously conceived and boldly executed piece of sustained imaginative fiction presented as historical fact. Geoffrey had succeeded as a historian even better than he could ever have hoped.

But from our point of view in this study of the Glastonbury Legends, even more important still was Geoffrey's utterly unforeseeable success as the originator of the greatest and most beautiful of all medieval romances, the cycle of stories known collectively as the Arthurian Legend, pure fiction and imagination unalloyed by any need to submit itself to the confining bonds of historical fact. The second half of the twelfth century, in so many different ways the 'great divide' of the Middle Ages, saw medieval man for the first time in command of the circumstances and conditions of his daily life. It witnessed the first realization of medieval ideals—the triumph of authority, order, law and justice over the forces of mindless greed and anarchy, and the emergence of religion, learning and art from the long night of barbarity which, in the West, had followed the decay of Rome and had come near to destroying civilization itself in the seven long centuries of strife which had ensued. Among the many manifestations of the new flowering of Western civilization which now became evident was the rise of the chivalric ideal among the noble and military classes of the Western kingdoms and principalities, a new ideal transforming the conception of knighthood from that of a mere human fighting machine into a loftier idea of a civilized and Christian warrior. Despite its intrinsic limitations and shortcomings, all too evident to us in an age of egalitarian democracy, the medieval chivalric ideal has long been one of the powerful influences moulding Western society and civilization from its most rapidly formative period in the late twelfth and early thirteenth centuries down to our own day.

At its origin in the second half of the twelfth century, the chivalric ideal meant the process of civilizing the still half-barbaric military aristocracy and warrior class which had necessarily dominated and set the tone of earlier medieval society. The new chivalric ideal was a strange, and at times even a fantastic compound, bearing in its nature much that was to prove extremely perilous to its more extreme devotees. It kept all the earlier insistence of the

heroic age on personal courage, skill in battle, and loyalty
to one's lord, but with these primitive virtues it blended
new qualities drawn partly from romance and partly from
religion. Thus it imparted into the very essence of knighthood something scarcely ever glimpsed, if at all, in the
earlier heroic and epic age—the love of men and women
for each other, in all of its degrees, physical, emotional and
finally even spiritual; and with this it also fused much of
pure Christian idealism, not only by incorporating Christian ideals of morality, but also by asserting that a true
knight owed duty and service to God and to the Church in
virtue of his knighthood. Truthfulness, just dealing, mercy
and forbearance to the vanquished, gentleness and protection for the weak and defenceless, and the quality of moral
courage which we call integrity and which they called
honour, were made no less essential parts of the knightly
ideal than the older, simpler, savage virtues which had
sufficed in the more primitive age. Few men could realize
the ideal of knighthood thus held aloft, but at its best it is
represented by Chaucer's 'very parfit gentil knight'—a
figure human enough, surely—by Sir Galahad of the fully
developed Arthurian Legend as Sir Thomas Malory was
to record it, and by the Chevalier Bayard, 'sans peur et
sans reproche'. It was the ideal of the gentleman, sharply
differentiated by his code of behaviour, 'courtesy', from
the mere mercenary soldier, and able to take his place
socially even with kings, earls and barons, for all of these
were essentially 'knights'. We know that the chivalric code
could often degenerate into merely fantastic excess and
into class rigidity, and that the inescapable contradiction
between the Christian and the romantic love elements in it
could lead to grave abuse and degenerate laxity of behaviour between men and women of noble birth. But here
what concerns us is the ideal, not the excessive actuality,

83

and the chivalric ideal of courtesy and of 'gentle' behaviour was the most potent instrument and expression of the civilizing of the medieval aristocratic warrior class.

The literary reflection of this decisive social and moral revolution was the change from primitive epic to medieval romance, which both expressed and shaped the new code of chivalric courtesy. The dual themes of the new literary mode, blended in varying proportions, were the romantic love of the knight for the lady of his devotion (be she married or single), and feats of heroic adventure in which the knight, seeking to win both renown among his fellows and favour in his lady's eyes, faced fearlessly strange and terrible perils and triumphantly overcame them. The adventure might, and usually did, include combat with ordinary human foes where the issue was decided by the skill and courage of the opposed knights, but it usually also held a greater or a lesser element of magic and terror in which the knight must strive against the dreadful superhuman powers of giants, ogres, monsters and wizards in seemingly hopeless encounters from which, nevertheless, he emerges victorious, though only after suffering grievous scathe. This supernatural element of magic and faery, sometimes helping the valiant knight or rewarding him with blissful days of restoration and happiness, but more usually confronting him with an adversary of terrifying aspect and daunting might, is an essential part of the romantic story, no less characteristic of it than the theme of the love between the knight and his lady. And throughout the romance the knight who is the hero of the story must display unfailingly the chivalric virtues of courage, moral now as well as physical, skill in horsemanship and in the wielding of his weapons, endurance unto death though sorely wounded, loyalty both to his lord and to his lady-love, good faith and truthfulness in all his dealings with his equals. He must be ready at an instant's call to succour the helpless and distressed, to rescue those whom he finds under oppression or in peril, especially if they be damsels or ladies—always assuming that they are of his own knightly class. He must be merciful, generous and courteous to all whom he meets (again, assuming that they are his social equals): he must hate evil and strive against it wherever he finds it: he must observe the universal duty summed up in the phrase 'noblesse oblige'—his status as a knight imposes this moral duty on him. And at all times he should remember that he is a Christian warrior, usually especially devoted to the service of Our Lady, the Queen of all women, though of course this is where practice and theory most commonly parted company. Thus did medieval romance first give shape and expression to the idea of a 'gentleman'.

To the writers of the later twelfth and early thirteenth centuries who first shaped these romantic stories, whether in poetry or in prose, the King Arthur of Geoffrey of Monmouth's *History* proved an inspiration beyond price. Perhaps if Geoffrey had never written they might, like the earlier epic writers, have fallen back on Charlemagne; but Charlemagne was too historical, too actual a figure for their romantic purpose, and far too much was known of him, his deeds and his time for him to serve as the central figure of their new world of imagination, the magical world of faery where anything could be made to happen, in complete disregard for the actual world of past and present fact. Arthur had been a real historic person, which gave to his story just enough of factual basis to serve the purpose of the romantic poets in creating an imaginative world just sufficiently, though tenuously, linked with reality to make their imagination not utterly incredible: but, apart from Geoffrey of Monmouth's fantastic 'History', nothing was known of Arthur to inhibit or restrain the imagination of the early romantic writers. It was not that they wished to make Arthur himself the subject and hero of their various romances: except when they told the superbly tragic and wonderful story of Arthur's last battle and of his marvellous passing, Arthur himself was not the hero of the story, nor his deeds its subject. They used Arthur and his 'plenary court' to furnish the centre, the ethos and the inspiration of the behaviour and the deeds of their many knightly heroes, and to give unity to the rapidly growing body of separate stories which they had to tell of exemplary heroes and of their marvellous adventures and their romantic loves. Just as in Geoffrey's *History* all knights and warriors who wished to achieve renown flocked to Arthur's court to profess themselves his vassals, so now, in the hundred years of the development of the medieval romance which followed immediately on the publication of Geoffreys' book, the poets and prose writers of this flowering age hastened to attach their hero-knights to the court of a King Arthur whom they speedily refashioned into a new and nobler guise than ever Geoffrey could have conceived for him. They endowed their King Arthur with virtues at which Geoffrey had never so much as hinted—all the virtues, in their most supreme form, of the rapidly-evolving code of chivalry—a transcendent love of justice, an infallible wisdom, a serene authority transcending merely human potential, so that Arthur became the very touchstone, the standard of chivalry, whose behaviour, judged by the code of courtesy, was beyond criticism, as his decisions were beyond question. His Court became supreme over the entire world of romantic story, having no human rival or neighbouring authority: only the supernatural elements in this world of imagination lay beyond his control and were usually hostile and malignant towards him and his knights, though even in this field, he was upheld by the superior magic of Merlin. The centre of his court became the famous 'Round Table' of the most valorous and chivalric knights of this world of imagination, few in number, carefully chosen, and all equal to each other but otherwise peerless even among Arthur's valiant followers. All young men of noble birth who wished to make names for themselves as true knights hastened to Arthur's court and sought acceptance as his vassals, aspiring to gain admission to the famed circle of the Round Table of chosen knights sworn to be eternally loyal to their glorious King, and to live and fight for his honour and for their own as befitted true knights seeking to realize in their lives and deeds the highest dictates of the code of chivalry. Thus was the Arthurian Legend created and refined out of the once-despised and neglected Celtic folk-memory and legend transmuted into new life by Geoffrey of Monmouth's 'fabled history'.

One preliminary process, however, was needed to make possible this second, unforeseen success of Geoffrey's Arthurian history. So long as Geoffrey's book remained available only in its original Latin, it was virtually closed to the laity, scarcely any of whom, in the twelfth century, could either read or understand Latin. But just as the chroniclers found in Geoffrey's *History* the full satisfaction of their own long-felt needs as recorders of the remote past and as exponents of the former glories of the British nation, so poets and prose writers, on both sides of the English Channel, realized that Geoffrey had written a story which the kings, nobles and knights of the new era would read or hear avidly if only it were translated into a language which they could understand—which, for most of them, meant French in one or another of its variant forms. This task was taken up almost immediately, and it may well be that before Geoffrey himself died in 1155, he had already learnt that Anglo-Norman translations of his book were being prepared by Robert Wace and Geoffrey Gaimar.

Other translations and paraphrases followed: about 1200 Layamon wrote the first 'Brut' in English, and speedily the fame of Geoffrey's work spread all over Western Europe, not only throughout England, Wales and France, but also into Germany and even into Italy and Spain, though these last two countries were little suited to the transplantation. By these means the aristocratic warrior-classes throughout Western Europe became familiar with the long story of early British 'history', and more especially with its Arthurian portion, which Geoffrey had devised with a complete understanding of the taste and mood of the men for whom he wrote. They cared little or nothing for its historical truth: unlike the Greeks and the Romans of classical times, they had very little sense of history as truth, and they brushed aside the denunciations of Geoffrey's scandalized historical critics, if indeed they were ever aware of these cries of protest from a mere handful of spoil-sport monastic scholars. Geoffrey had given them history as they wanted it to be, and his translators had put it into words which they understood. By the time of Geoffrey's death it was already a matter of reproach to be unfamiliar with his story, and well before the turn of the century it was as much the staple diet in the literary education of the aristocracy as ever was Virgil for the young Roman or Homer for the Greek.

It was this process which enabled the French romance-writers of the later twelfth and early thirteenth centuries to develop the full-blown Arthurian Legend from Geoffrey's crude story of Arthur, his court, his knights and his victories. Marie de France seems to have begun the process, but it was Chrétien de Troyes who did most to develop the 'matter of Britain', as Geoffrey had provided it, into the great cycle of Arthurian romances, and Chrétien was followed by several other poets, and by prose-writers too, throughout the next fifty years. The development came by adding new stories to the original core of the story of Arthur (itself rapidly transmuted to accord with the new conceptions of chivalry): new stories from Welsh, Breton, and purely French sources, but so transformed and adapted by the imaginative genius of the French writers that the Arthurian cycle lost nearly all of its Celtic character and became the very flower of medieval French literature, French in ethos no less than French in language, no matter whence the original germs of its many stories had been taken. And such was the cultural supremacy of France and of the French language as the common international tongue of the military aristocracy over all Europe west of the Rhine, that this Arthurian cycle of romance, with all the new stories, new characters and new atmosphere given to it by the French poets, rapidly became no less the possession of the English and the German aristocracies as well, and in turn both German and English stories were added to the stock. The Arthurian Legend reached its full growth as an international cycle of romantic stories of King Arthur and his knights, a cycle of polished and even sophisticated tales far removed both in substance and in character from the original raw conceptions of Geoffrey of Monmouth, and embodying, by 1250, all that was best and most characteristic in the contemporary chivalric code and all that was imaginatively ethereal in the new romantic spirit.

It was because the chivalric code and the romantic ideal had both come to maturity in a Christian society and even, in some measure so far as the code of chivalry was concerned, under the aegis of the Christian Church during the very height of its influence and power over the minds of ordinary men, that, well before the middle of the thirteenth century, the endless quest for the Holy Grail had been imported into the Arthurian cycle, to give it both a moral and religious objective and a recurrent underlying unity. The Holy Grail, the sacred cup used by Christ and the Apostles at the Last Supper, and subsequently hidden and lost to human ken, became the ultimate objective of a quest in which all of the knights of Arthur's Round Table were engaged. It was a quest which would continue until at length one of Arthur's knights, the only utterly pure and faultless man among them, should discover the Grail and so, in some way unexplained by the poets, bring about the millennium in which all Christian souls would at last turn wholly to God. It is significant that the romances reserved the discovery of the Grail to a knight—not to a cleric, no matter how saintly, still less to any layman of lower birth and rank. It was the poet's addition to the general Arthurian theme, and not the direct work of the clergy and the Church. The Church, indeed never formally accepted or gave any official recognition to the story of the Grail, for its vague and loose poetical conception carried with it dangerous heretical implications which accorded ill with the strict theological system which the Church had by this time worked out. So however much individual clerics, themselves often sprung from noble and knightly families, might be seduced by the wistful and romantic magic of the legend of the Holy Grail, the Church never gave it official countenance, and it remained, despite its Christian inspiration, a concept of laymen devised for the perfection of a cycle of poetic romances, and essentially the possession of the knightly class. Popular imagination seized upon this inspired addition to the Arthurian Legend, regarding it as a coping stone to the whole structure, and whatever the Church might or might not officially decide, popular imagination had its way, and the story of the quest for the Grail became an essential part of the Arthurian Legend.

For several centuries more, both the *Brut* and the Arthurian Cycle of romance were to continue their development, all the time exercising powerful influences upon English poetry and imaginative prose. The *Brut*, challenged only ineffectively until, in the sixteenth and early seventeenth centuries, first Polydore Vergil and then William Camden exposed mercilessly its fictitious character, continued long as the genuine and accepted early history of the British people, and through Holinshed's *Chronicle*, which popularized 'the British history' as no earlier work had done, it also provided both inspiration and themes for the Tudor dramatists, including Shakespeare himself. As for the Arthurian Legend of the romances, Sir Thomas Malory's *Morte d'Arthur* made it fully and finally the property of the English people above all others, even the French, and gave to the Arthurian Legend its most coherent and fullest expression. It inspired Edmund Spencer, and three hundred years later it was still powerful enough to move Alfred Tennyson to his most sustained and haunting poetry, and to inspire the pre-Raphaelite painters with many of their favourite themes. Even to-day it still lives for us, in any of its manifold versions, for we still live ourselves in the romantic age, debased and degraded though most of our modern 'romance' may be, and the old magic of the medieval romancers still has power to put its spell upon us. But for the argument of this book, we need go no further than 1250, the latest possible date for the final revised version of William of Malmesbury's *De Antiquitate*. We can sum up, for our present purpose, this long digression on Geoffrey of Monmouth's *Historia Regum Britanniae* and on the early development of the Arthurian romantic cycle by saying that, although Glastonbury had not been so much as mentioned by them, Geoffrey and his translators and paraphrasers had made the history of King Arthur and his victories the common knowledge of the aristocracy and chivalry of both England and France, and that well before 1250, the whole Arthurian Legend, the supremely noble and all-powerful King, his lovely Queen Guinevere, his court, his knights of the Round Table embodying all that was best in the contemporary chivalric ideal, and finally, their quest for the Holy Grail, had become the greatest and most widespread theme of the brilliantly flowering literature of the age. The stage was set for the return of Arthur and for the birth of the Glastonbury Legends.

VI

THE ARTHUR OF the romantic cycle was King of a
faery kingdom which had no location in either time
or place, for it was a kingdom of pure fantasy and
imagination. But the King Arthur of Geoffrey's *History* and
the *Brut* was presented as the ruler of the kingdom of Britain in the first half of the sixth century, and the date of his
'passing' was given definitively as A.D. 542. Presumably,
therefore, the various places mentioned in the *History*, the
sites of his capital and court, and of his many battles and
sieges, should all be capable of identification with specific
cities, towns, fortresses and other places in Medieval Britain. Inevitably men began to speculate on the truth in
the Legend, to try to locate the scenes of Arthur's battles,
the site of his castle and court, the realm where he had
reigned, the place where he had been dealt his mortal
wound, the Isle of Avalon to which he had at last been
borne away. Then, with a shock of surprised delight, the
literate Western world learned in 1191 that the grave of
Arthur and Guinevere had been discovered at Glastonbury.
The date 1191 is given by Ralph of Coggeshall, a very
careful contemporary chronicler who is not likely to have
been mistaken, but the fullest account of the discovery, the
significant account for our purposes, is provided by Gerald
of Wales in his *De Instructione Principis*. In a long passage
which was probably written in 1193, reporting a visit
which he had very recently made to Glastonbury, he gives

93

us what might be described as an eye-witness account, at one remove, of the startling discovery. So let Gerald speak for himself and for Glastonbury.

'Now the body of King Arthur, which legend has feigned to have been transferred at his passing, as it were in ghostly form, by spirits to a distant place, and to have been exempt from death, was found in our own days at Glastonbury, deep down in the earth and encoffined in a hollow oak between two stone pyramids erected long ago in the consecrated graveyard, the site being revealed by strange and almost miraculous signs; and it was afterwards transported with honour to the Church and decently consigned to a marble tomb. Now in the grave there was found a cross of lead, placed under a stone and not above it, as is now customary, but fixed on the under side. This cross I myself have seen, for I have felt the letters engraved thereon, which do not project or stand out, but are turned inwards towards the stone, They run as follows:

'Here lies buried the renowned King Arthur,
with Guenevere his second wife,
in the Isle of Avalon'.

Now in regard to this there are many things worthy oi note. For he had two wives, the last of whom was buried with him, and her bones were found together with his, but separated from them as thus; two parts of the tomb, to wit, the head, were allotted to the bones of the man, while the remaining third towards the foot contained the bones of the woman in a place apart; and there was found a yellow tress of woman's hair still retaining its colour and its freshness; but when a certain monk snatched it and lifted it with greedy hand, it straightway all of it fell into dust. Now whereas there were certain indications in their writings that the body would be found there, and others in

94

the letters engraven on the pyramids, though they were
much defaced by their extreme age, and others again were

Lead cross found in King Arthur's grave. Camden, 1607

given in visions and relations vouchsafed to good men and
religious, yet it was above all King Henry II of England
that most clearly informed the monks, as he himself had
heard from an ancient Welsh bard, a singer of the past,

that they would find the body at least sixteen feet beneath the earth, not in a tomb of stone, but in a hollow oak. And this is the reason why the body was placed so deep and hidden away, to wit, that it might not by any means be discovered by the Saxons, who occupied the island after his death, whom he had so often in his life defeated and almost utterly destroyed; and for the same reason those letters, witnessing to the truth, that were stamped upon the cross, were turned inwards towards the stone, that they might at that time conceal what the tomb contained, and yet in due time and place might one day reveal the truth.

Now the place which is now called Glaston was in ancient times called the Isle of Avalon. For it is as it were an isle, covered with marshes, wherefore in the British tongue it was called 'Ynys Afallon', that is 'the apple-bearing isle'. Wherefore Morgannis, a noble matron and the ruler and lady of those parts, who was, moreover, kin by blood to King Arthur, carried him away after the battle of Camlan to the island that is now called Glaston, that she might heal his wounds. It was also once called 'Ynys gutrin' in the British tongue, that is, 'the glassy isle', wherefore when the Saxons afterwards came thither they called that place 'Glastingeburi'. For 'Glas' in their language has the same meaning as 'vitrum', while 'buri' means 'castrum' or 'civitas'.

You must also know that the bones of Arthur thus discovered were so huge that the words of the poet seemed to be fulfilled:

'And he shall marvel at the huge bones in tombs his spade has riven' (VIRGIL, *Georgics*, i, 497).

For his shank-bone when placed against that of the tallest man in that place, and planted in the earth near his foot, reached, as the Abbot showed us, a good three inches above his knee. And the skull was so large and capacious as to be a portent or a prodigy, for the eye-socket was a good palm in width. Moreover, there were ten wounds or more, all of which were scarred over, save one larger than the rest, which had made a great hole'.*

Gerald adds a little to this story in a later version of it in his *Speculum Ecclesiae*. He tells us that the monk who snatched so greedily at the golden tress of hair in the coffin over-balanced and fell into the hole, emerging all covered with mud and clay—an early object-lesson for amateur archaeologists on the need for delicacy and restraint in recovering finds! We learn here, too, that the Abbot who showed Gerald the tomb and the relics was Henry de Sully (Soilli), who was Abbot of Glastonbury from 1189 to the autumn of 1193, and was consecrated Bishop of Worcester on 12 December 1193, which fixes the date of Gerald's visit to Glastonbury as not later than the summer of 1193. When Gerald saw it, the new tomb prepared in the Church for Arthur's body had been completed and the body had been transferred to it, which suggests that, if the body was found in 1191, the date of Gerald's visit could hardly have been very much before the end of 1192.

It was this sensational discovery which transformed the Glastonbury tradition and was the real beginning of the two-fold Glastonbury legend as we have it to-day. Arthur's grave had at last been found, and found, most appropriately, in the burial-ground of the Abbey which William of Malmesbury had already hailed as the first spring and fountain-head of the Christian faith in Britain, a beginning which the Glastonbury tradition, in its more extreme form, already carried back to the first Christian century and to an Apostolic origin independent of Rome. And to clinch the matter, the burial cross hidden with the coffin declared the

* H. E. Butler (edit. and trans.). *The Autobiography of Giraldus Cambrensis*, pp. 119–21.

identification of Avalon with Glastonbury, and Gerald, in reporting it, was the first writer to publish that identification, which he did in most explicit terms. It is true that Gerald did not mention the Holy Grail or Joseph of Arimathea; but the unequivocal, unchallengeable identification of Avalon with Glastonbury, so clearly made by the leaden cross, and so plainly and learnedly expounded by Gerald of Wales, was decisive. With the development of the Arthurian Legend in the later twelfth and the early thirteenth century, the Saint was dragged in the wake of the Hero: Arthur had come to Glastonbury, so Joseph of Arimathea must come too, bringing with him the Holy Grail which was eventually to be buried in Chalice Well centuries later. The new version of the Glastonbury Legend, now incorporating both St. Joseph and King Arthur in its claims, quickly superseded the old: William of Malmesbury's monograph no longer covered the accepted facts, and so the *De Antiquitate Ecclesiae Glastoniae* had to be rewritten to accommodate the latest results of recent research and archaeology. The economically-minded monks, however, had no wish to waste the valuable asset of William's name, and so they rewrote his book for him, modestly making no claim whatsoever as the editors and revisers of a minor, but not unimportant work of a great historian of the previous century.

VII

WE CAN NOW answer the questions 'When?' and 'How?' concerning the birth of the Glastonbury Legends: 1191, by the discovery of the skeletons and the leaden cross in the monks' cemetery. We are left with the question 'Why?'.

On 25 May 1184 fire broke out in the Abbey and destroyed all of the buildings except a bell-tower and a single chamber: the *Vetusta Ecclesia* was destroyed with the rest. The community was stunned: so terrible was the disaster that the shock and dismay of it still echoed in the pages of Adam of Domerham, the official continuator of the history of the Abbey, writing 100 years later, a little before 1290. But the community had good friends: on hearing of the calamity, Henry II headed the subscription list, in response to a national appeal, by magnificently instructing his Chamberlain to devote to the rebuilding of the Abbey all of the unexpended balance of the year's royal revenue remaining in his hands: one hopes that the royal account was not overdrawn! The monks themselves hastened to do all that might be expected of them in such a crisis: they exhumed from the burnt-out ruins the relics of famous saints long dead—Patrick, Gildas, Indraht and others, and even discovered that they possessed the body of their former Abbot and re-founder, Dunstan—much to the indignation of the monks of Christchurch, Canterbury, where the saintly Archbishop's body had lain in peace for over two hundred years. These venerable relics they deposited in shrines where they might attract the generous gifts of pious worshippers: some they sent on a begging tour, carried by monks well-provided with indulgences. The response was most gratifying; following the King's lead, wealthy nobles and ladies began to subscribe, and even though the monks were without an Abbot, (for the Abbey was in the King's hands during an excessively prolonged vacancy which had begun in 1178), the chapter made plans for rebuilding the Abbey on a vast scale that would match its glorious pretensions: the new Church alone was to be 400 feet long. How good was the response and how energetic the chapter's recovery can be judged from the fact that in 1186 they were able to dedicate the new Church of St. Mary, the Lady Chapel as it came to be called, built on the same axis as the destroyed *Vetusta Ecclesia*, below the west end of the vast new church which they planned. The new Lady Chapel, a lovely and gracious building even in its present ruined state, was begun in the late Norman Transitional style, which was almost immediately changed into a masterly Early English, possibly the work of the great but anonymous architect who had introduced it at Wells Cathedral about 1180, soon after its first use by William de Sens in the rebuilding of Canterbury after their great fire of 1174. The size and the beauty of the ornamentation of the Lady Chapel, no less than its novel style, are all indications of the worthy ambitions of the chapter for their new Abbey. Then evil fortune smote again; in 1189, with only the Lady Chapel finished and work on the great church barely begun, Henry II, their generous patron and benefactor, died. The blow was even more cruel in the sequence, for the new king, Richard I, was not in the least interested in building churches for homeless monks, no matter how venerable their tradition: he wanted all the money he could get for his Crusade. Most of the nobles followed the royal lead again, and the appeal fund dried up almost overnight. The position at Glastonbury once again became desperate. Something drastic must be done, and quickly.

In this crisis some unknown monk must have come forward with a suggestion which marks him out as a genius who would have made his fortune in a modern advertizing agency. By a brilliant stroke of imagination he proposed a superb advertizing stunt—'Find Arthur's tomb!'. To an age which read far more avidly of King Arthur and his Queen, his knights of the Round Table and their treacherous foes, than it read of the whole calendar of saints, the impact of such a discovery would be tremendous, the appeal irresistible. In the golden age of forgery, here was the master-forgery of all! Perfectly timed and staged, on any grounds other than those of morality and religion it deserved to succeed, and succeed it did, and has gone on succeeding down to our own day.

What, then, were the two skeletons unearthed at Glastonbury in 1191 and shown so impressively to Gerald of Wales afterwards? The skeletons were real enough, but they certainly were not those of King Arthur and Queen Guinevere of the medieval romances, for they were creatures, not of the flesh but of the lightest and most delicate fantasy, who never lived nor died to be buried in the heavy earth, but are immortal and imperishable in imagination. Nor was it the real Arthur who was found there, the Arthur of history, whose mighty achievements we can but faintly discern through the dense mist of the Dark Ages, and whose place in the last age of sub-Roman Britain the late Professor Collingwood so recently and so discriminatingly attempted to recover for us. For the Arthur of history was not a king, but simply a country gentleman, a self-made leader of armoured cavalry who, like Oliver Cromwell, won imperishable glory as the champion of his country in its hour of need, somewhen early in the sixth century. Nothing in history is known to link this Arthur with Glastonbury, though we must remember that this is the darkest of all ages in British history and that we know extremely little of the real Arthur. It would, in these circumstances, be folly to assert that the Arthur of history never visited so holy a shrine as Glastonbury had become by his lifetime, especially if we prefer the opinion that south-western England, not Wales or Brittany, was the main scene of his activities, and that, as the 1966 excavations tend to suggest, Cadbury Castle may have been his base-camp. As for his burial place, who knows where he lies? The Welsh said that he had never died: 'A grave there is for Mark, a grave for Gwythwr, a grave for Gwgawn of the Red Sword: a mystery till the Day of Judgment the grave of Arthur', said one Welsh poet.

What, then, were the Glastonbury skeletons? Had the monks, by an amazing stroke of luck, perhaps while digging a grave for one of their community, accidentally unearthed a genuine Celtic burial in its original site? Or had they, as seems much more likely, salted their mine in preparation for the 'discovery'? Had the clever publicity-agent of the chapter suggested to the new Abbot, Henry de Sully, that it would be a good idea to transplant into the Abbey graveyard, behind the secrecy of screened excavations, the remains of some prodigious but nameless Celtic chieftain and his wife, buried, more than 1,000 years earlier, in one of the dug-out canoes which used to rock gently by the wooden landing-stage at the causeway of the prehistoric lake-village in the swamp below the Tor? They may, even, conceivably have been victims of the dreadful massacre of the villagers by the Belgae shortly before the Romans came. Adam of Domerham, writing the official history of the

Abbey about 100 years after the great discovery of 1191, tells us that the Abbot Henry 'on a certain day set curtains round the spot and gave orders to dig'; it would be an odd detail for Adam to have introduced into the story unless it were true. But whoever it was whose skeleton they found, it was not the Arthur of history, for he was never a king; but he was a Christian, and the 'hollow oak', or dug-out canoe, which enclosed the two skeletons, hardly looks like Christian burial.

The leaden cross, intended to be so convincing, is the feature which most clearly gives away the forgery. When Gerald saw the cross, it had presumably been detached from the stone—if ever it had been fastened to it—for he was able to read the inscription. It is a peculiar thing that, of several writers who at different times have reported the inscription on the cross, Gerald alone (and those who can be shown to have copied what Gerald wrote) includes the words 'with Guinevere his second wife'—neither Ralph de Coggeshall nor Adam of Domerham reports them. One wonders whether Gerald invented them to improve his story—he liked a good story—or whether his memory played him false? The cross itself was real enough, for the Tudor antiquary Leland, visiting these parts *c.* 1542, says that he had it in his hands and examined it carefully: he gives its height as about one foot. In describing Arthur's tomb, between those of King Edward the Elder and Edmund Ironside, in the presbytery of the Church, to which Arthur's remains had been finally translated with impressive pomp and ceremony when Edward I visited Glastonbury in 1278, Leland says that the cross was on the tomb—or at least, this is the meaning usually attached to his rather cryptic note, '*Crux super tumulum*'. Camden also saw it, and reproduced a drawing of the cross, with its antique inscription, in the 1607 edition of his *Britannia*. Both Leland

and Camden reproduce the wording of the inscription in the same words as Gerald of Wales, but without the reference to Guinevere. The cross itself disappeared late in the eighteenth century. He would be a very rash man who would assert that the lettering, as reproduced by Camden, is in a sixth-century script! But actually, lettering apart, the wording gives the fake away as a twelfth century improvisation going back no further than the point in the development of the Arthurian Legend at which Arthur came to be thought of as a King.

As for Gerald's two 'stone pyramids', which appear also in the accounts given by Ralph of Coggeshall and Adam of Domerham, they too were real enough. They were presumably the tapering shafts of two square stone crosses which had lost their heads—crosses of the Celtic and Anglian type common in the lands of the Celtic Church and in those parts of Northern and Midland England which had been evangelized by Celtic influence. William of Malmesbury had seen them and had deciphered fragments of the inscriptions. What he reported of these does not bear out Gerald's suggestion that the inscriptions indicated Arthur's burial place; they suggested to William the names of abbots, bishops and princes, both British and English, buried there. The shafts were still standing in position as late as 1777.

Why—apart from the obvious necessity of the Abbey precincts being Arthur's burial-place if the new buildings fund was to benefit from the discovery—did Abbot Henry decide on a spot between the two 'pyramids' as the site of the excavation? Ralph of Coggeshall's account makes the discovery 'accidental': he says that the skeletons were found when a grave was being dug for one of the monks who had specially begged to be buried between the two 'pyramids', though it hardly seems likely that the gravediggers would have 'dug to an immense depth', until they 'were almost in despair', as Adam of Domerham says, and that they would have reached the depth of sixteen feet, as Gerald's account implies, if all they had intended to do had been to dig a grave for one of the brethren. The official story, as told to Gerald by Abbot Henry, and recounted one hundred years later by Adam of Domerham, was that King Henry II (who had visited St. David's in 1171) had learnt from a Welsh bard, well-versed in the history of his nation, that Arthur's body would be found 'at least sixteen feet beneath the earth, . . . in a hollow oak', and that Henry had therefore urged the monks of Glastonbury to have a search made in the Abbey grounds. Gerald does not actually say that the bard had mentioned the two 'pyramids', or the monks' graveyard, or even Glastonbury or indeed any other named spot: but Glastonbury had claimed, throughout the twelfth century at least, to be the oldest Christian site in Britain; its church and cemetery were crowded with ancient burial-slabs, as William of Malmesbury tells us, and the two 'pyramids', with their barely-legible accumulation of names of ancient abbots, bishops and princes, Celtic as well as English, were probably the likeliest signposts in all England for anyone proposing to dig for Arthur's tomb with no more precise indication than that afforded by the supposed prophecy as Gerald reports it. Henry II had indeed some reason to wish Arthur's body found: Wales was, for the time being, peaceful under the powerful domination of the Lord Rhys, who was on very good terms with Henry, recognising Henry's suzerainty: but Welsh politics were never stable for long, and too much depended on Rhys' life and goodwill. Should Rhys die or quarrel with Henry, Wales might yet again flare up in dangerous rebellion, and the career of Owen Gwynedd had shown how Welsh passions might become heated to a point approaching an outburst of nationalism, even in those early days. Welsh pride was powerfully stimulated by poetic appeals to former glory, and the Welsh believed that their Arthur had not died, but lay waiting in an enchanted sleep in some unknown place, until the hour should strike when he would come forth to lead his people to victory once more, and sweep the accursed English out of the land. A widespread belief such as this, skilfully exploited in troubled times, might set an imaginative and poetic nation aflame, if a pseudo-Arthur should appear, to call the men of Wales to revive their ancient glory. Much better, from Henry's point of view, that the legend of the immortal Arthur should forever be given the lie by finding Arthur's tomb and proving it to be no cenotaph! So Abbot Henry did well to father on to the departed Henry II the idea that search should be made for Arthur's tomb, and where better, in all England, could search be begun than between the two enigmatic but portentous 'pyramids' in the most sacred place in the holiest and most ancient Christian site in Britain? We need look no further for obscure traces of folk lore or tradition which would link the names of Arthur and of Avalon with Glastonbury before 1191: the ancient tradition of Glastonbury itself, as recorded by William of Malmesbury, is sufficient. And as for the other factors which, as Gerald was told, had prompted the Abbot's decision, the 'visions and relations vouchsafed to good men', and especially to 'religious', in the twelfth-century use of that term, do not constitute evidence which the mere historian can handle; and 'certain indications in their writings' is not a form of reference which enables us to check the sources of the story.

Grievous though the loss be, we must therefore dismiss Arthur, whether as hero or as king, from any proven historical connection with Glastonbury: the legend linking him with the Abbey springs entirely from the 'discovery' of 1191 in circumstances which proclaim the find a most ingenious but blatant fraud to raise money for a most praiseworthy purpose—the rebuilding of Glastonbury Abbey. And with Arthur must go 'Pomparlès', the 'Bridge Perilous', a name traced no farther back than 1415—though in any case it would require a very powerfully stimulated imagination to believe that Excalibur lies hidden in the shallow stream that flows beneath the bridge to-day.

We must, however, be careful not to deny that the Arthur of history ever visited or had any connection with Glastonbury, especially now that preliminary press reports have been published giving the general results of the excavations carried out during the summer of 1966 at both Cadbury Castle and Glastonbury Tor. Meagre as such reports must necessarily be, they make it clear that strong evidence was found to confirm the local tradition that Arthur used Cadbury Castle as a base-camp, and to suggest that he may have used Glastonbury Tor as a signal-post. To attempt to identify Cadbury Castle with 'Camelot' is, of course, a fundamental error: 'Camelot' is part of the wholly imaginary world of the Arthurian romantic cycle, and has even less factual and historical basis than the 'King Arthur' of the romances himself. 'Camelot' is nowhere to be found in terms of geography. Nor should we expect that these or any further excavations at either site will positively and specifically prove that it was the historic Arthur who made use of them. Proof of that kind could come only from coins or inscriptions indisputably attributable to the early sixth century and expressly naming Arthur, and such finds are beyond the bounds of expectation or even of possibility. So far as we know hitherto, no coins minted in Britain early in the sixth century have ever been discovered at any site whatsoever, nor, apart from a few examples in the Irish 'Ogam' script, have any inscriptions of this period ever been found in England. Archaeologists and historians have therefore concluded that well before the beginning of the sixth century, coins had ceased to be minted in Britain, and that the Roman habit of inscription on tombstones, memorial slabs, altars, foundation and dedication stones and the like had also perished with Roman rule. For the early sixth century, therefore, the archaeologist expects to find only artefacts which tell him nothing of individual men and women by name, however much light they can be made to throw on the way in which life was lived then—material, economic and social facts, and even, by bold deduction, some general conception of the political affiliations and structure of whole communities. The expert can date this material approximately, give or take half a century, especially if it is found associated with material of Continental origin to which a still closer dating can be assigned. But of named individuals, living in this particular period, the first half of the sixth century, the archaeologist can tell us nothing directly, and he does not expect to be able to say more at any foreseeable future time: civilization in Britain had crumbled too much for any such evidence to be expected.

Even so, the 1966 excavations at Cadbury Castle and on Glastonbury Tor have undoubtedly strengthened greatly the possibility of associating both of these sites with the historic Arthur. At Cadbury Castle, Mr. Leslie Alcock's team found abundant evidence that the Iron Age hill fortress, like many others in Southern England, was strongly re-occupied for a prolonged period during the 'Dark Age' which followed the collapse of Roman rule in Britain. While the nature of the material discovered makes precise dating, such as is often possible to the archaeologist dealing with Romano-British finds, quite impossible at Cadbury Castle,

Mr. Alcock reports confidently that his discoveries prove that a large encampment existed at Cadbury Castle in the sixth century, and that the finds are 'absolutely characteristic of the Arthurian period.' The excavations of the summer of 1966, conducted for the Camelot Research Society Committee, were preliminary only: they lasted for only two weeks, and uncovered only a small part of the eighteen-acre site, so that for any final verdict on Cadbury Castle we shall obviously have to wait for several years more, until the Committee has been able to commission a complete excavation of the whole site, and Mr. Alcock has then had time to present a full report on all the material found there.

Nevertheless, Mr. Alcock's preliminary findings have already aroused the widest interest, not merely among archaeologists and historians, but also among the general reading public. It is not too much to say that he has already shown that the local belief that Cadbury Castle was Arthur's headquarters has some solid basis in historical and archaeological fact, even though, of course, no material identifying Arthur by name can be expected in these finds. What Mr. Alcock discovered can be summed up very briefly as pottery and metalwork, including a bronze cloak-pin, an iron knife-blade and other material which Mr. Alcock attributes to the sixth century, and, more significant, post-holes, some of them more than a foot in diameter, indicating that large wooden buildings were erected here in the 'Arthurian' period. Such buildings must mean a prolonged re-occupation of the site: and moreover, large quantities of meat-bones were also found, and some of the pottery was identified as fragments of large wine-jars imported from the Continent and coming originally from the Eastern Mediterranean. Altogether, especially when we remember that only a small portion of the site has yet been excavated, it seems to have been already proved beyond reasonable doubt that in the sixth century a powerful British leader, wealthy enough and still sufficiently civilized to have kept some of the habits of Romano-British civilization, and to have been able to import from the Continent (if only from Gaul), wine contained in jars of East Mediterranean origin, reoccupied Cadbury Castle in force with a large band of warriors, and erected within the ramparts residential buildings of a more or less permanent character. Mr. Alcock makes no assertion that this leader was the historic Arthur, but he quite fairly says that 'the site would give us the image of an Arthur-type figure'; and that, short of finds utterly beyond the expectation of any archaeologist working with material of this period, is as far as we can go with certainty. It is, in fact, a very long way!

At the same time, Mr. Philip Rahtz was completing a three-year excavation on the top of Glastonbury Tor, and his discoveries reinforce strongly the Cadbury Castle findings. Once again, the excavators found large quantities of meat-bones and fragments of sixth-century East Mediterranean jars which had once contained wine and olive oil. The occupation of this site, too, was obviously prolonged, and Mr. Rahtz suggests that it may have been used as a signal-station, linked with Cadbury Castle to the south, with Brent Knoll, at the western end of the Mendip Hills, to the north, and thence across the Severn Estuary to another sixth-century British camp at Dinas Powis, in the Silurian country of South Wales. We should remember that it was not until after the Battle of Dyrham in A.D. 577 that the Saxons were able to drive a wedge separating the British territories in Wales from those in south-western England, so that until well after the middle of the sixth century, co-operation between the British on both sides of the Severn Estuary was presumably still very close and well-coordinated. It is significant that after the end of the sixth century the encampment on Glastonbury Tor came to an end, and that no further evidence of re-occupation of the site before the late Saxon period, about the end of the tenth century, was discovered. These late tenth and early eleventh century finds suggested a small religious community, whether of monks or of hermits, and this also seems to have come to an abrupt end, after which there was no further re-occupation of the site until late in the thirteenth century, when the now ruined church was built on the summit of the Tor, with what seems to have been a well-equipped priest's house, with glazed tiles and good window-glass, maintained by Glastonbury Abbey until the Abbey itself was finally and tragically dissolved in 1539.

Thus, from two quite separate sites, we have strong evidence of the establishment in the sixth century in West Somersetshire of a strong and well-organized military force maintained over many years, with Cadbury Castle as its possible headquarters, and led by 'an Arthur-type figure' who still kept up something of the Romano-British way of life, and was still able to trade with the Continent, even if only as far as Gaul, for supplies essential to that way of living. While the archaeologists would not expect to be able to identify this leader by name as Arthur, in all the mixture of scanty history and plentiful legend which has come down to us from this dimly-discerned period, Arthur's is the only name that would fit this role. Thus it seems probable, to say the least of it, that if we accept Collingwood's carefully argued and discriminating thesis of a genuine historical Arthur living and fighting in south-western Britain early in the sixth century, Cadbury Castle was at least one of his principal fortresses and possibly his headquarters. It would not be in the front line of defence, for that was still far away to the north-east, probably no nearer than the downs overlooking the Vale of the White Horse and the Kennet valley, thanks to Arthur's decisive victory at Mons Badonicus, wherever that elusive site may be. We may therefore imagine Cadbury Castle as Arthur's rear base and permanent headquarters, from which the defence of the distant frontier against the encroaching Saxons could safely be organized and directed, with the aid of a chain of signal stations like that on the summit of Glastonbury Tor. All this seems to fit in well with Collingwood's Arthurian hypothesis, put forward thirty years ago. The only big question which the new evidence raises is that of Arthur's status. Was he, as Collingwood argued from his close reading of the text of Nennius, simply a Romano-British country gentleman, a *decurio*, to use the Roman technical term, who, more intelligent and resolute than any other of his contemporaries, grasped the tactical significance of the heavily-armed cavalry force introduced into the Roman Army in the late Imperial period, and therefore gathered together and equipped a strong cavalry force of trained and disciplined 'Ironsides', and led them successfully, in the service of any British king who had the heart to fight against the Saxons of the upper Thames valley, seeking to push ever deeper into south-western Britain? Or was he, after all, as tradition asserts, himself a King, perhaps ruling over a kingdom big enough, sufficiently peopled, civilized and organized enough to construct the massive eighty-mile rampart of Wansdyke to block the Saxon advance from the Thames and Kennet valleys on to the chalk downs and Salisbury Plain? Collingwood himself postulated the survival, at the end of the fifth century, of such a kingdom: was Arthur its ruler and perhaps even the man who conceived and organized the building of Wansdyke, or at least a close successor of that king? In either case, his use of heavy cavalry for attack and of strongly entrenched fortresses for defence against a foe who fought on foot and used the tactics of persistent infiltration warrants Collingwood's description of him as 'the last of the Romans in Britain', and won for him his unique place in both history and legend.

Cadbury Castle, looking out over the whole forested and swampy valley to Glastonbury Tor and beyond, was but a dozen miles' ride from Glastonbury, and there can be little doubt that a Celtic monastery had been established at Glastonbury by Arthur's time. Assuming, as we must, that Arthur was a Christian, it would be unreasonable to suppose that he never visited the primitive little abbey which lay within sight of his headquarters. But as for his burial-place, who knows where that may have been? The one certain thing is that it was not in the dug-out canoe which the monks found in 1191, buried sixteen feet below the ground, between the two 'ancient pyramids' in the Abbey cemetery. Mr. Lewis Thorpe, the recent translator of Geoffrey of Monmouth's *History*, hints that he may have found Arthur's real resting-place on the banks of the River Camel (Camlan) far away in Cornwall. But the best opinion is still that of the Welsh poet—'a mystery, to the Day of Judgment, the grave of Arthur'.

VIII

MORE GRIEVOUS STILL, the Holy Grail vanishes with Arthur's expulsion from the scene: it never had any historical substance, but was pure myth and fantasy, grafted on to the Arthurian Legend at a fairly early stage well before 1240, and flourishing greatly on that powerful stock. To be fair to the monks of Glastonbury, they never claimed to have the Grail, nor gave countenance to the belief that Joseph had brought it with him. The Church rightly mistrusted the romantic myth of the Holy Grail—as employed in the romances, it smacked too much of magic, and so, in spite of its religious element, the Church never gave formal recognition to the belief in the Holy Grail. What the Glastonbury monks said was that Joseph had brought with him two 'cruets', stoppered vessels resembling tall, slender jugs, the one containing the blood, the other the sweat of Christ at his Passion, and that these 'cruets' were not mysteriously hidden by Joseph before his death, but were buried with him in his tomb, wherever that might be. They may be seen portrayed in the late fifteenth or early sixteenth-century glass in the east window of Langport Church, nine miles away under Ham Hill, where St. Joseph is shown carrying the two 'cruets' on a white cloth in his right hand; or again, carved on the wooden chancel screen at Plymtree in Devon, where the saint holds one 'cruet' in each hand. Richard Bere, the penultimate Abbot of Glastonbury (1494–1524) made great

114

use of, and may even have devised, the heraldic shield
bearing a cross between the two 'cruets', which one historian of Glastonbury has scornfully reduced to 'R. Bere's
fanciful arms, a cross between two beer-flagons', on the
analogy of many another such punning rebus-device of the
later middle ages. On the sixteenth-century coat-of-arms of

St. Joseph's Arms. Window in St. John's Church, Glastonbury

St. Joseph in the south window of St. John's Church,
Glastonbury, the two 'cruets' appear in the lower quarters
of the shield on either side of a green cross notched like the
trunk of a tree shorn of its branches—St. Joseph's staff
which became the Glastonbury Thorn—with blood-drops
falling across all four quarters of the shield. The late Dean
Armitage-Robinson also recorded four stone representations
of the shield in or near Glastonbury, three of them being
on buildings erected by Abbot Richard Bere. The Grail
does not seem to have been represented on any medieval

carving or in any medieval glass that has survived in the neighbourhood of Glastonbury.

Much more grievous is the disappearance of St. Joseph of Arimathea himself. Transplanted to Glastonbury early in the thirteenth century along with the rest of the newly-localized Arthurian legend, Joseph, like his famous staff, has flourished mightily under our varying skies, far from the land of his birth. Not merely the first evangelist of Britain, the founder of Glastonbury, the planter of the Glastonbury Thorn, the builder (by proxy) of the *Vetusta Ecclesia*, and the bringer of the 'cruets' and the Grail, he has become, in modern times, a wealthy Jewish merchant importing tin into Palestine from the Cornish tin-mines before ever the Romans conquered Britain, and there are those who believe that he sent his 'nephew', Jesus, to Cornwall, while Jesus was still a young lad, to look after the Cornish end of his 'uncle's' business. This, we are told by the enthusiasts for the more extreme forms of the Glastonbury legend, is why we hear nothing in the New Testament of Christ's adolescence and earliest manhood: and it was during this long period of exile that Christ came to Glastonbury, and with his own hands built the *Vetusta Ecclesia* under the Tor, for Joseph and his disciples to discover when they at length arrived at Ynys Gutrin, as the revised version of the *De Antiquitate* tells us.

In the fulness of time St. Joseph was buried at Glastonbury and so joined the countless throng of the Abbey's saints—probably in the later thirteenth century, and certainly before 10 June 1345, when one John Blome obtained from the chancery of Edward III a letter patent licensing him, provided he could obtain the permission of the Abbot and convent, and could conduct his search without harm to them or to their church and houses, 'to dig within the precinct of the said monastery and to seek for those precious relics . . . the venerable body of the noble decurion Joseph of Arimathea, which rests in Christ buried within the bounds of the monastery of Glastonbury, and is to be revealed in these days to the honour of God and the edification of many.'* Apparently John Blome asserted that 'a divine injunction has been laid on him concerning (Joseph's body) . . . to wit, that he should seek it diligently until he find it, because it is said to be contained in certain ancient writing that his body was there buried.'* Therefore Edward III (or if not Edward in person, then his Chancellor, writing doubtless in his capacity as keeper of the king's conscience), 'desiring to pay devout honour to his sepulchre and to the relics of him who performed such offices of religion and humanity to our Redeemer in His death, taking down his body from the cross and laying it in his own new sepulchre; and hoping for ourselves and all our realm a wealth of grace from the revelation aforesaid',* gave to John Blome the licence for which he had petitioned. The magic of the Glastonbury Legend was already powerfully at work, convincing not only earnest-minded visionaries, but even a worldly-minded King and his presumably hard-headed Chancellor. In our own day Shakespeare's tomb has been opened on a pretext no more plausible than that advanced by Blome in 1345.

We do not know whether Blome ever got the Abbot's permission to begin his inspired search, or whether he, or the monks themselves, ever started to dig for Joseph's tomb. An anonymous East Anglican chronicler, connected with Peterborough and Spalding and writing late in the fourteenth century, records baldly under the year 1367 that 'the bodies of Joseph of Arimathea and his companions were found at Glastonbury'. But Glastonbury itself never

* These three quotations are from J. Armitage Robinson, *Two Glastonbury Legends*, pp. 53–64.

claimed to have found St. Joseph's body: there persisted at the Abbey a strong tradition, to which John of Glastonbury, who rewrote and greatly expanded the history of the Abbey late in the fourteenth century, bears emphatic witness, that Joseph had been buried 'on a two-forked line' near the south corner of the *Vetusta Ecclesia*. Although this belief was repeated by William of Worcester late in the fifteenth century, and has other echoes elsewhere, right down to the time of the Dissolution the monks of Glastonbury were uncertain whether St. Joseph's body lay within their walls or not. Long after the Reformation, William Good, a Jesuit exile in Italy who had been born at Glastonbury in 1527 and who, as a boy, had served Mass at St. Joseph's altar there, recorded that 'the monks never knew for certain the place of this saint's burial, or pointed it out; they said the body was hidden most carefully, either at Glastonbury or on a hill near Montacute, called Hamden Hill, and that when his body should be found, the whole world should wend their way thither on account of the number and wondrous nature of the miracles worked there.'* In fact, miracles worked by St. Joseph had already been recorded at the beginning of the sixteenth century: the crypt of the Lady Chapel had become known as St. Joseph's Chapel (a name later extended to the Lady Chapel itself), and an image of St. Joseph had been placed there by Abbot Chinnock in 1382, and speedily this Chapel of St. Joseph became a place of pilgrimage and intercession, where many miraculous cures were reputed to have taken place. By the end of the middle ages, Joseph of Arimathea, completely Anglicized and at home, had become Glastonbury's greatest asset.

Yet, if we are to write in terms of history, Joseph, like Arthur must go: he must go because Arthur has been expelled, and he came in Arthur's wake, but appreciably

* Armitage-Robinson, *op. cit.*, p. 46.

later, and he had come because Arthur had been found at Glastonbury, though not until, in the first half of the thirteenth century the Holy Grail had become an integral part of the Arthurian legend. We must be careful of the words we use: we may not flatly assert that Joseph never came to Glastonbury, for this is one of those negatives which cannot be proved. After all, we know next to nothing of Joseph of Arimathea: he figures very briefly and incidentally in the Gospels at the Crucifixion and the Resurrection, and that is all we know of him, unless we accept the later story, in the so-called Gospel of Nicodemus, which tells of his arrest and imprisonment by the Jews in Jerusalem after the Crucifixion; and of his miraculous release by divine intervention. Nothing in all this links Joseph of Arimathea with Britain, Gaul or even with the Apostle Philip: his association with Philip and his leadership of a first-century mission of evangelization to Britain are first recorded in the final, 1240/50 version of the *De Antiquitate*. It is an extremely late tradition, beginning nearly 1100 years after the events which it purports to narrate, and we have seen how it came about. Yet it is well to reflect that, thanks to the *Pax Romana* and, after 43 A.D., to the Roman conquest of Britain, a wealthy Jew, especially if he happened to be a merchant, could have travelled more easily from Palestine to Glastonbury in the thirty years following the Crucifixion than at any later time until well into the nineteenth century. Strictly speaking, it is not impossible that Joseph of Arimathea came to Glastonbury: historically speaking, there is not a scrap of evidence whatsoever to support the tradition that he did so come. Anyone who believes this tradition must believe it as an act of faith, and not as a fact established or even suggested by historical evidence or reasoning.

In his *King Arthur's Avalon*, Mr. Geoffrey Ashe has made

the interesting and by no means implausible suggestion that the introduction of Joseph of Arimathea into the Glastonbury Legend really stands for the presence at Glastonbury, about the middle of the first century A.D., and possibly even before the Roman conquest of Britain, of some highly civilized and wealthy Jew or Syrian who had migrated from his homeland to settle in a remote place, perhaps, at the time of his coming, beyond the boundaries and the power of the Empire. Such an exile, Mr. Ashe suggests, might have built himself a villa of Roman type at Glastonbury, and, supposing him further to have been a Christian, might even have erected some sort of Christian oratory in which to practise his Christian faith, without seeking native converts. From such a beginning, obscurely remembered in folk-tradition, the legend of Joseph of Arimathea and the *Vetusta Ecclesia* might have sprung many centuries later. It is an ingenious idea which cannot be dismissed out of hand. But no trace of such a settlement has yet been found at Glastonbury: the nearest Roman villa yet discovered lies below the Polden Hills, some three miles away. Until Roman remains, demonstrably of the middle of the first century, and large enough to support the suggestion of a wealthy Levantine exile, have actually been unearthed at Glastonbury, Mr. Ashe's idea must remain mere conjecture: in any case it does not bring Joseph of Arimathea back into the history of Glastonbury.

Joseph takes away with him 'Chalice Well', a purely modern identification, probably of the late eighteenth century, when mention of a healing well first appears: and after all, the Holy Grail has not been found there, although there are many who believe passionately that it is now in a country mansion, Nanteos, three miles from Aberystwyth in Cardiganshire. The owners of Nanteos have long preserved a much worn and damaged fragment of a wooden vessel, known locally as 'the Healing Cup of Tregaron', and often claimed to be the Holy Grail itself. The story is that the monks of Glastonbury, on learning that their Abbey was about to be dissolved, hurriedly sent the Grail to the far-off Abbey of Strata Florida in Cardiganshire for safe keeping, and that after Strata Florida too had been dissolved, the Cup came eventually into the hands of the Nanteos family and has there remained ever since. It is widely believed to have healing powers, and hundreds of sufferers from various diseases and disabilities have begged to have sent to them water which has been poured into the Healing Cup; such requests still continue to be received and are never refused, though the strict rule, always observed, is that no payment may ever be accepted for this healing service. Belief in the Cup is evidently strong and widespread and is by no means confined to Wales. Yet it must be remembered that the Glastonbury monks never claimed to possess the Holy Grail or to have known anything of it. Why, in any case, the monks of a great Benedictine Abbey in England should have sent so precious a treasure as the Grail (supposing them to have had it) to a small and, by that time, very decadent Welsh Cistercian Abbey having no known connection with Glastonbury, it is difficult to imagine—especially as Strata Florida was dissolved in the same year as Glastonbury!

'Wearyall Hill' goes too: it still had not been so identified in the sixteenth century, and in fact this version of the name is simply a pleasant bit of folk-etymology, for early forms of the name show it to have been 'Wirrall' Hill—'the hill of the bog-myrtle meadow'—a very likely name for a place so situated. 'Ynys Witrin', as the revisers of the *De Antiquitate* spelt it, or 'Ynys Gutrin', in Gerald's version, may indeed be translated, as Gerald translated it, into 'Insula Vitrea'; but 'vitrum' means 'woad', as well as 'glass' or 'mirror', and the English name 'Glastonbury' embodies the Celtic element 'glas', which means 'blue', the colour of woad dye, or an old Celtic derivative of that adjective, meaning 'woad'—a plant which flourishes in marshy places. Gerald's 'Ynys gutrin' may very well be no more than his own Anglo-Welsh etymology based on the assumption that the 'Glas' of Glastonbury means 'mirror'; and Professor Ekwall, after stating the possibilities, concludes that 'the meaning would be "place where the woad grew."' As for the Glastonbury Thorn, there is no miracle about that, beyond the yearly miracle of all plant life: it is merely a well-known, though not a common botanical 'freak', which flowers, not indeed annually on Christmas Day—after all, what happened to it in 1752, when the famous 'eleven days' were dropped from the calendar?—but simply out of season in the winter-time, and it is offered for sale to-day in nurserymen's catalogues. The Thorn, too, is a late invention: it is first mentioned in writing early in the sixteenth century, though it appears on a fourteenth-century seal of the Abbey, where the Virgin holds it in her hand.

We must reject too, not only the story of Joseph of Arimathea's leadership of the mission of evangelization, but the whole episode of a first century mission at all. William of Malmesbury tactfully discredited it and we shall do well to follow his example. It is an older tradition than that which brought either Arthur or Joseph of Arimathea to Glastonbury—older by at least a century, but it will not do. As William said, if we can believe that Philip the Apostle really did evangelize Gaul, then there is no inherent improbability in the idea that he may have detached a second mission thence to convert Britain. Freculfus, whom William learnedly cited, did not originate the story that Philip was the evangelist of Gaul, for that statement can be traced back to Isidore of Seville, writing early in the seventh century: but neither Freculfus nor Isidore mentions a further mission to Britain at that time. Actually, tradition (though not Scripture) makes St. Philip the apostle, not of Gaul (Gallia), but of Galatia in the Northern part of Asia Minor, 'Gallia' may be a simple mistake for 'Galatia', on the part of St. Isidore or some still earlier writer, or it may be that some independent-minded Gallic prelate, eager to assert the independence of the Church of Gaul from growing Papal claims in the fifth or the sixth century, and wishing therefore to assert a separate apostolic foundation of the Church of Gaul which should owe nothing to St. Peter or to his Roman successors, picked upon St. Philip to be the apostle of Gaul because 'Galatia' could colourably be misrepresented as 'Gallia'. There is no independent historical evidence whatsoever for the conversion of Gaul, or of any known part of it, still less of Britain, to Christianity at so early a date as A.D. 63. The attribution of the origin of Glastonbury, as a Christian community, even without St. Joseph, to the first century cannot be traced farther back than the mention of the story by William of Malmesbury c. 1130, though it may have been in circulation for some little time then. After all, the entire story of the first-century mission under St. Joseph, and of the re-establishment of the community by St. Phaganus and St. Deruvianus in the time of Pope Eleutherius and King Lucius, is said by the revisers of the *De Antiquitate* to be derived from the 'charter of St. Patrick'—a most dubious source, especially when we consider that the charter which they used was a duplicate, thoughtfully provided by St. Patrick at the time of the original 'charter', and stored for safety in the Chapel of St. Michael on top of the Tor, where it providentially escaped the destruction of documents in the Abbey library in the great fire of 1184.

We must, moreover, remember that the excavations conducted by Mr. Philip Rahtz on the summit of the Tor apparently discount completely the story that any kind of ecclesiastical community was maintained there before the late tenth century. Such occupation of the site as there was before then was evidently a purely military encampment of the sixth century, after which the summit of the Tor remained deserted until, approximately, the time of St. Dunstan. St. Patrick's charter, with its anachronistic indulgences, was obviously a most blatant and preposterous forgery, even down to the impudent reference to the apocryphal 'Wellias', St. Patrick's companion on the Tor, introduced to support Glastonbury in its long struggle against the Bishop of Wells by suggesting that his see was founded, as a daughter-church, by a monk from Glastonbury. Clearly, this would not have been the document which William of Malmesbury had seen: he had been shown whatever the library had contained about 1130, a very different document from the 'charter' of St. Patrick cited by the revisers of the *De Antiquitate*. What sort of document that was we are not likely to discover now, but it did not satisfy William, and it should not satisfy us, who cannot now inspect it. It might, even so, have been a very old document, conceivably going back to a forgery made in the seventh century by some Welsh cleric determined to assert an origin independent of Rome for the Welsh Church during the struggle against the haughty pride of St. Augustine and his successors, whose argument of Papal authority might be countered by showing that British Christianity derived, not from a Papal mission of the late second century, but from an independent apostolic mission only thirty years after the Crucifixion.

If we then reject, as historically we must, the idea of a mission from Gaul in A.D. 63, can we accept William of

Malmesbury's story of a second-century conversion by unnamed missionaries sent by Pope Eleutherius at the request
of Lucius, a king then ruling over, or at least in, Britain?
Not as it stands, even when we recall how careful William
is to give no detail of which he feels uncertain. There was
no King Lucius, nor any other kind of king, in the Roman
province of Britain near the end of the second century—and
there is no suggestion that the dominions of Lucius lay
beyond the Wall or across the Irish Sea. William is simply
mistaken, that is all. He was a very careful historian, with
a sound critical attitude to the sources which he used—his
rejection of the story of the first-century mission shows that.
But historians generally, sooner or later, reach a point
where they have to take on trust the statements of other
historians: one cannot check everything. In such circumstances, all that the trusting historian can do is to make
certain of the general reliability of the writer whose statements he proposes to reproduce. William did that: he tells
us that 'annals of good credit' are the source which he
employed for this part of his history of Glastonbury. So
they were: on whom better than the Venerable Bede could
William, writing when he did, have relied for information
about the early history of Christianity in Britain? The story
is given very briefly in the fourth chapter of Bede's *Ecclesiastical History of the English Nation*, and we cannot reasonably
blame William for accepting that work as being 'of good
credit'. Bede, too, was a most scrupulous and careful historian: he too erred in good faith, for this story almost certainly was based directly upon information which he received from Rome itself in response to his urgent requests
for any documents or other information which might throw
light on the early history of the Church in Britain. To have
to rely on someone else's transcripts or notes of inaccessible
source-material is surely one of the worst quandaries in

which a historian may be placed, and Bede was let down by his Roman correspondent, who, following the official *Liber Pontificalis*, is usually supposed to have misread as 'Britannia' the word 'Birtha', generally identified with the Castle of Edessa in Northern Mesopotamia—a very far cry from Glastonbury! The explanation is at least plausible and is generally accepted, though not proved. At any rate, Bede was misled, and so he in turn misled William of Malmesbury and generations of historians after him.

Does anything at all remain, then, of the Glastonbury legends after this work of destruction, almost as deplorable as that of the great fire of 1184, is done? Something still remains, something worth preserving, even if it cannot be entirely proved, for the heart and core of William of Malmesbury's story may still be true, at least in its general sense. William, good historian as he was, undoubtedly believed many things of Glastonbury which we to-day would find unacceptable for belief. We need not believe with William's revisers, that St. Patrick re-founded the Glastonbury community as a monastery in A.D. 432 or at any other date, or that he ruled there as Abbot in his closing years: we need not believe that any one of the saints whom William or the revisers name from the Celtic period of Glastonbury actually visited Glastonbury, still less that any particular one of them lived there and did the various things which the *De Antiquitate* narrates, such as St. David's mistaken attempt to consecrate the *Vetusta Ecclesia* and his building of a second church at Glastonbury when he discovered his error. Yet the Celtic saints were great travellers, and while nothing whatsoever can be proved, there is nothing inherently impossible, or even improbable, in the idea that many of the great men and women of the Celtic world came to visit Glastonbury at some time in their lives, that some of them may have lingered there, and some even have died there: these things may or may not have been true. Gildas and David sound by no means unlikely visitors to Glastonbury: Patrick and Bridget are perhaps somewhat less probable: Columba is perhaps the most unlikely of the many saints whom the revisers name. The story that St. Patrick first organized a monastery at Glastonbury in A.D. 432 is probably an over-precise and mistaken recollection that the first true monastic community was organized by Irish missionaries working in south-western England in the sixth—not the fifth—century, and the inclusion of the names of Bridget, Benignus and other Irish saints in the Glastonbury roll merely a way of recording the activities of Irish missionaries in this field for a period of some 200 years. An earlier community of unorganized hermits may, or may not, have existed at Glastonbury before the Celtic missionaries first organized a monastic house there. But one fact is clear: when the English arrived at Glastonbury soon after 658 they found a great and famous Celtic monastery already established and flourishing there, a monastery already venerated as the holiest place in Britain, with a primacy in time springing from great antiquity stretching back to a lost origin before firm history begins in this part of the land. No other house in Britain, either then or at any later time, claimed such a primacy or sought to wrest from Glastonbury the proud boast of being the first and the oldest religious house in Britain. Though we reject the story of a first-century mission of Christianity to Britain, William's—and Bede's—story of a mission sent late in the second century may not be very far from the truth. Early in the third century Tertullian claimed that Christ had conquered parts of Britain inaccessible to Roman arms, and before 250 Origen referred to Christianity in Britain in such a way as to suggest that it had established itself there strongly. In view of this, the last two or three decades of the second century are by no means an impossibly early period for the arrival of Christianity in Britain.

We reject the story of the arrival of St Joseph and his companions in A.D. 63 as completely unhistorical: yet even so the legend may enshrine one almost forgotten truth. It tells us that the disciples came from Gaul, presumably from Armorica since their landfall was in the West, and that they approached Glastonbury from the west: may not this be a very significant fact embedded in the mass of fancy? At this point the prehistory of the Glastonbury area once more becomes relevant. We should remember the economic importance, both before and for some forty years after the beginning of the Christian era, of the thriving community of craftsmen and traders living in the lake villages of Glastonbury and Meare, and we should keep in mind the well-developed trade-routes which they established. One of these followed the coasts of Somerset, North Devon and Cornwall west and south-west to Armorica. The lake-villages were destroyed by the Belgae shortly before the Romans arrived in these parts, but established routes are apt to persist in use for ages after the trade which created them has dwindled and decayed. Traders from Western Gaul, and especially from Armorica, still continued to use this old route as the way to the relatively rich and civilized lands of the Dobunni to the south and east of the Severn Estuary, and Glastonbury, even at the end of the second century A.D., was still not very far from this western sea-route. Scholars in recent years have familiarized us with the idea that Christianity may first have reached these islands, not by the easy and obvious short sea-route to Dover and London, but, like so many earlier cultures and and some religions of the pre-historic age, in the little boats of traders and adventurers braving the stormy western approaches between the Armorican and the Cornish coasts.

We cannot prove it, and probably we never shall: but if we accept this idea as a possibility, is there anything incredible in the thought that, coming from the south-west, and along the south coast of the Bristol Channel, it was under Glastonbury Tor that Christianity found its first secure shelter and abiding-place in our remote land?

BIBLIOGRAPHICAL NOTE

SOURCES

1. (i) William of Malmesbury's original account of Glastonbury, as written in the second edition (*c.* 1140) of his *De Gestis Regum Anglorum*, was edited by William Stubbs in the *Rolls Series* (2 vols., London, 1887–9): it has been translated into English by John Sharpe, *The History of the Kings of England and the Modern History of William of Malmesbury* (1815): by J. A. Giles, *William of Malmesbury's Chronicle of the Kings of England* (Bohn's Antiquarian Library, London, 1847), based on Sharpe's translation; and by Joseph Stevenson in *The Church Historians of England*, Vol. iii, pt. i (London, 1854).

   (ii) William's *Vita Sancti Dunstani* was edited by Stubbs in *Memorials of St. Dunstan*, (Rolls Series, London, 1874). His *De Gestis Pontificum Anglorum* was edited by N.E.S.A. Hamilton (*Rolls Series*, 1870); an earlier edition appears in Migne's *Patrologia*, clxxix, 1441–1680 (Paris 1855).

   (iii) William's *De Antiquitate Glastoniensis ecclesiae*, in its finally altered form of *c.* 1240, was first edited, very unsatisfactorily, by Thomas Gale in *Scriptores*, *XV*, pp. 289–335 (Oxford 1691); a rather better, but still imperfect edition was produced by Thomas Hearne in his *Adami de Domerham Historia de rebus gestis Glastoniensibus*, i, 1–122 (Oxford, 1727); and it appears also in Migne's *Patrologia*, clxxix, 1681–1734 (Paris, 1855); a modern, critical edition of this text is much to be desired.

2. Adam of Domerham's *Historia de rebus gestis Glastoniensibus*, 1126–1290, written by the sacristan of the

130

Abbey near the end of the thirteenth century, was edited by Thomas Hearne in Vol. ii of the Glastonbury collection which Hearne published under that title (see previous paragraph).

3. John of Glastonbury's late fourteenth-century text, beginning with the earliest times, abridging Adam's history for the period 1126–1290, continuing the story thence, and finally continued late in the fifteenth century by another Glastonbury monk taking the story very briefly down to 1493, was also edited by Thomas Hearne, *Johannis Glastoniensis Chronica sive historia de rebus Glastoniensibus*, (2 vols., Oxford, 1726).

4. William Good's sixteenth-century account of Glastonbury, in Latin, was edited by Archbishop Ussher in his *Britannicarum ecclesiarum antiquitates* (Dublin, 1639) and reprinted in his *Whole Works* (Dublin, 1847–64): the portion relevant to this book was reprinted by Dr. J. Armitage Robinson, *op. cit.*, app. VI. (see below).

5. Geoffrey of Monmouth's *Historia Britonum* was edited by J. A. Giles (Caxton Society, London, 1844), and translated by the same in *Six Old English Chroniclers* (Bohn's Antiquarian Library, London, 1848). Mr. Lewis Thorpe has recently published a lively translation of Geoffrey's *History*, providing it with an admirably comprehensive introduction and detailed notes, a most useful time-chart tabulating Geoffrey's chronological equations with events outside British history, and an excellent index which is in fact a concise summary of all that Geoffrey says about each person or place mentioned in the text. There is also a very helpful bibliography: *Geoffrey of Monmouth's History of the Kings of Britain*, trans. Lewis Thorpe (*Penguin Classics*, Penguin Books, Harmondsworth, 1966). Sir Thomas D. Kendrick, *British Antiquity* (Methuen, London, 1950) is much the most useful account of the development and influence of the

Brut from Geoffrey of Monmouth's time to the seventeenth century.

6.   Gerald of Wales' accounts of the 1191 excavations are printed in his *De principis instructione* and his *Speculum Ecclesia,* edited by G. F. Warner and by J. G. Brewer respectively, in vol. viii and vol. iv. of *Giraldi Cambrensis Opera (Rolls Series,* London, 1861–1891); the passage from the *De principis instructione* was translated by Professor H. E. Butler in *The Autobiography of Giraldus Cambrensis,* (London, Cape, 1937).

SECONDARY WORK

Much the best recent book on the subject is by the late Dean of Wells, Dr. J. Armitage Robinson, *Two Glastonbury Legends: King Arthur and Joseph of Arimathea* (Cambridge University Press, 1926), which embodies articles and conclusions previously published by the author in periodical and in essay form. The great debt which this present account owes to Dr. Robinson's book will be obvious to anyone using the latter, and is gratefully acknowledged by the present writer. One of the most valuable features of Dr. Robinson's book is the number of extracts, whether translated or in Latin, from original sources not always easily accessible even though printed.

Another highly valuable work is a long article by William Wells Newell, 'William of Malmesbury on the Antiquity of Glastonbury', *(Publications of the Modern Language Association of America),* xviii (1903), 4, pp. 459–512, which is much concerned with the discussions of the subject by students of the history of medieval literature and legends, and which prints long and useful Latin extracts of significant passages from the sources.

There are shorter and more popular accounts, though still of scholarly and reliable quality, by the late Dr. Montagu R. James, in *Abbeys*, (London, G. W. R., 1925) and by E. Foord, *Wells, Glastonbury and Cleeve* (*Cathedrals, Abbeys and Famous Churches Series*, edited by G. Home, London, Dent, 1925). A very brief summary of the main facts is given by the present writer in a broadcast talk subsequently printed in *Myth or Legend?* (edited by Glyn Daniel, London, Bell, 1955).

The following works provide useful background reading for various aspects of the subject or of related themes:

Prehistory: Grahame Clark, *Prehistoric England* (London, Batsford, 1945) provides the most detailed information about the lake villages of Glastonbury and Meare.

Stuart Piggott, *British Prehistory* (Home Univ. Library, Oxford University Press, 1949).

Jacquetta Hawkes, *A Guide to the Prehistoric and Roman Monuments in England and Wales* (London, Chatto and Windus, 1951).

Jacquetta & Christopher Hawkes: *Prehistoric Britain* (Pelican Books, Harmondsworth, 1942).

Roman Britain: R. G. Collingwood and J. N. L. Myres, *Roman Britain and the English Settlements to about 600 A.D.* (*Oxford History of England*, i, Oxford University Press, 1936)—useful for the prehistoric lake-villages also.

Anglo-Saxon England: Sir Frank Stenton, *Anglo-Saxon England* (*Oxford History of England*, ii, Oxford University Press, 1943)

R. H. Hodgkin, *A History of the Anglo-Saxons* (Oxford University Press).

P. Hunter Blair, *An Introduction to Anglo-Saxon England* (Cambridge University Press, 1956).

Anglo-Norman England: A. L. Poole, *From Domesday Book to Magna Carta* (*Oxford History of England,* iii, Oxford University Press, 1951).

Glastonbury Abbey: David Knowles, *The Monastic Order in England,* (Cambridge University Press, 1941).

  N. Pevsner; *South and West Somerset* (*The Buildings of England,* Pelican Books, Harmondsworth, 1958), gives a succinct account of the architectural development of the Abbey, and is useful for the prehistoric lake-villages also.

William of Malmesbury: Stubbs's prefaces to the *De Gestis Regum Anglorum* and to the *Memorials of St. Dunstan* (see under SOURCES) and K. R. Potter's preface to William's *Historia Novella* (*Nelson's Medieval Texts,* London, 1955), can be supplemented by W. de Gray Birch, 'Life and Writings of William of Malmesbury', in *Transactions of the Royal Society of Literature,* New Series, vol. x, (London, 1874).

Early Church History: L. Gougaud, *Christianity in Celtic Lands* (London 1932), N. Chadwick, Kathleen Hughes, Christopher Brooke and Kenneth Jackson, *Studies in the Early British Church* (Cambridge University Press, 1958), especially C. Brooke, 'The Archbishops of St. Davids, Llandaff, and Caerleon on Usk'.

  E. G. Bowen, *The Settlements of the Celtic Saints in Wales* (University of Wales Press, Cardiff, 1954).

Bibliography: G. Ashe, *King Arthur's Avalon* (London, Collins, 1957), though somewhat diffuse and, by strict historical standards, rather uncritical, has a considerable and very useful up-to-date bibliography which discriminates usefully among the countless books and pamphlets, some of them highly unscholarly, which have appeared on this topic.

  The useful select bibliography in Mr. Lewis Thorpe's translation of Geoffrey of Monmouth's *History,* not only opens up the literature on Geoffrey's book itself, but also affords an introduction to modern work on the growth of the Arthurian Legend. Sir Thomas Kendrick's *British Antiquity* has full and invaluable bibliographical references in its footnotes.

I have not attempted to deal with the vast body of literature tracing the literary sources, variants, analogies and ramifications of the Glastonbury Legend, as beyond the point to which they are taken in this present essay, they have little bearing on the historical aspects of the subject, however scholarly some of them may be.

For the growth and development of the Arthurian Legend, the best general introduction is E. K. Chambers, *Arthur of Britain* (London, 1927; reprinted with supplementary bibliography, 1965).

INDEX

Date Due

MR 06 '78			
MR 6 '78			